T0330958

Food, Philosophy, and Intellectual Property

This is a book about food, philosophy, and intellectual property rights.

Taken separately, these are three well-known subjects, but it is uncommon to consider them together. The book comprises 50 case studies, organized around eight themes: images; genericity and descriptiveness; language traps; procedures; menus, recipes, and creativity; boundaries; biotech; and empowerment. The introductory chapter frames the selection of cases and encourages readers to look beyond them, envisaging new lenses to look at food vis-à-vis intellectual property. The terrain encompassed is wide-ranging and reaches out to fine-grained aspects of food products, recipes, and cooking. Conceived for a wide scope of readers, the volume ultimately interrogates the links between food and cultural identity, bringing to the fore the ethical, political, and aesthetic worth of culinary arts and gastronomic experiences.

This accessible book will be of value to scholars, students, practitioners, and others with interests in the areas of intellectual property, food law, and food studies.

Enrico Bonadio, Reader in Law at City, University of London, UK.

Andrea Borghini, Associate Professor in the Philosophy Department at the University of Milan, Italy.

Food, Philosophy, and Intellectual Property

Fifty Case Studies

Enrico Bonadio and Andrea Borghini

Routledge
Taylor & Francis Group
a GlassHouse Book

First published 2024
by Routledge
4 Park Square, Milton Park, Abingdon, Oxon OX14 4RN

and by Routledge
605 Third Avenue, New York, NY 10158

Routledge is an imprint of the Taylor & Francis Group, an informa business

A GlassHouse book

British Library Cataloguing-in-Publication Data
A catalogue record for this book is available from the British Library

ISBN: 9781032560649 (hbk)
ISBN: 9781032560656 (pbk)
ISBN: 9781003433675 (ebk)

DOI: 10.4324/9781003433675

Typeset in Times New Roman
by Deanta Global Publishing Services, Chennai, India

Contents

Foreword

Michael T. Roberts
(Professor of Policy and Executive Director,
Resnick Center for Food Law and Policy,
University of California, Los Angeles,
UCLA School of Law)

My approach in this Foreword is to reflect on my journey in food law and policy as it relates to this book. I hope this approach sets the table for appreciating an excellent book by Professors Enrico Bonadio and Andrea Borghini that demonstrates the rich potential of this discipline.

The Journey to Food Law and Policy

When I taught the first Food Law and Policy class in the United States some 20 years ago, I wrestled with the question of what is food law and policy? Is it a discipline? If so, what are its boundaries? I answered these questions later to some extent in a treatise titled *Food Law in the United States*. To be sure, there is a statutory framework, at least in the United States, which started with the 1906 Pure Food and Drug Act,[1] was formed mainly by the 1938 Federal Food, Drug, and Cosmetic Act, and has been further shaped by several amendments to this act. But food law and policy, at least in my view as noted in the treatise, has a broader framework tethered not as much to a set of laws or rules as it is to the modern food system(s), unlike anything the world has ever seen given its consequences, complexity, and globality.

Within this framework, food laws and policies apply to problems and issues arising from the components of the modern food system(s), such as food production, processing, packaging, marketing, distribution, and consumption. These issues involve numerous stakeholders, from the farmer to the consumer, and beckon the use of various legal tools. Translated into academic language, food law and policy are multi-doctrinal. They implicate health law (food safety, labeling, and nutrition public policies), environmental law (agriculture production inputs, land and water use, climate change), international law (international standards for food and animal products, trade, and market

---

1 Not to be forgotten is the 1907 Federal Meat Inspection Act, which conferred jurisdiction for various activities related to meat and poultry on the United States Department of Agriculture.

access), tort law (product liability from food safety incidents), constitutional law (speech issues from labeling and advertising restrictions), property law (zoning to restrict fast food restaurants and farmland ownership), and tax law (farm succession and small farm policy). This list barely scratches the surface, as evidenced by this book and its expansive food and intellectual property (IP) coverage.

With such a broad application, a fair question is whether food law is not a discipline in and of itself but merely a subsection of other forms of law. To quote from my treatise:

> the case to consider food law as a discipline (albeit multidoctrinal) in and of itself is strong. Its value lies in focusing attention on how the law governs the food from the field to the table […] by recognizing how the law governs food, improvements can be made, and dynamics can be better understood.
>
> Roberts 2016, p. 10

To complete my reflection on this journey, I conclude from my experience as a scholar and a former legal practitioner in this space that what distinguishes the effective food law lawyer is their understanding of food systems—what they are and how they work—and how law itself can be a systems approach intersecting with other disciplines, policies, norms, and cultural dynamics within the food systems. Above all else, the effective food law lawyer and scholar thinks holistically even when operating in a fragmented modern food system.

Encountering this Book

This book comports nicely with my journey's vision of what constitutes food law and policy. I support this claim briefly in the following four observations about the book.

Intellectual property: pivotal and expansive area of food law and policy. The future of food is both food and technology. Hence, IP issues abound and will continue to increase in food law. Even assuming this premise, the breadth and scope of this book's coverage of IP issues in food is impressive. In their discovery of this rich "legal jungle," as put forth by the authors, the reader can sense and share with the authors an appreciation for the vastness of issues and tensions, as exhibited by the tension between product aesthetics and value in the German case study involving chocolate squares. Who would have guessed before reading this book that 50 legal disputes and case studies could be organized under eight IP topics? After reading the book, one realizes that we have only scratched the surface of IP issues in food, now and in the future.

Interdisciplinary and multidoctrinal. The power of the interdisciplinary approach in food law is in full force in this book. There is no way that the eight unique categories of food and IP could be fully fleshed out absent the book's theoretical and practical IP framework inspired by philosophy. This framing and infusion of philosophy makes essential questions more accessible, especially those involving justice and fairness. From start to end, where the new food IP challenges are discussed—from robots in the kitchen to restaurant non-fungible tokens to virtual restaurants—the book pounds home very effectively that IP issues in food, whether in the past, present, or future, are laden with symbolism and values. This constancy gives this book a long shelf life.

Systems focused and grounded in cultural relevance. The book is also a powerful reminder of how culture matters regarding food and strongly influences how food is governed politically or in courts. When teaching food law and policy to students, I start the first class by asking students to share family recipes (assuming the student's grandmother is willing to share the recipe, which does not happen regularly) or meaningful experiences with a food product that speaks to their heritage. This exercise aims to develop the notion that what we think about food—a commodity, cultural value, or a combination—can dictate our position on policy issues and normative conflicts regarding food. This book takes this simplistic classroom strategy to a new level of sophisticated analysis, providing nuanced thinking for effective food systems and problem-solving strategies, evidenced in the Ethiopian coffee case study where trademark protection disputes gave way to a partnership between the Ethiopian government and the US coffee giant Starbucks.

Fruitful scholarship. It is rewarding to witness scholarly publications like this book requiring us to think in new ways about the intersection of law and food. Instead of harmonizing a complicated application of law to food and IP, the authors create an inventory of issues via case studies to invite comparisons and a rethinking of food and IP. This wise course generates a constructive dialogue among stakeholders that is integral to food systems thinking. What should be especially exciting for food law scholars is that the book is organized to create links with scholarly conversations, including those about food sovereignty, food justice, food security, and other ethical, political, and cultural aspects of food throughout the supply chain. Finally, the book's bottom-up approach creates possible bridges between different disciplines—law or otherwise—and fosters creativity and holistic thinking.

I was sold on the idea of this book when I first heard about it. Now, after reading the book and immersing myself in rich and exciting case studies contextualized by legal and philosophical analysis, I am completely converted to this approach.

Source

Roberts, M.T. (2016). *Food Law in the United States.* Cambridge University Press.

Preamble

This is a book about food, philosophy, and intellectual property (IP) rights. Taken separately, these are three well-known subjects, yet it is uncommon to consider them together. In fact, to the best of our knowledge, this is the first book to explicitly do so.

The idea of the volume grew out of conversations and exchanges between the two of us—Enrico, a legal scholar specializing in IP law, and Andrea, a philosopher specializing in food issues. Our views on the subject matter developed in very different milieus, addressing apparently unrelated topics. But, when we first met in the Fall of 2018, we realized that our respective areas of expertise complemented each other and could be fruitfully merged to close some gaps in the literature.

As we compiled and selected case studies for this volume, we came to agree that the most urgent scholarly contribution was not from a meta-ethical or political perspective. As we delved into the "legal jungle" of court litigations, out-of-court disputes, and simple case studies over food and IP across the globe, any idealistic notion of justice was torn apart by the myriads of legal systems, caveats, and perspectives. The issue is not only a matter of professional intricacy: philosophies around the world can hardly be seen as harmonious, and one would struggle to find philosophical principles and ideals shared globally. Of course, laws should be just and fair. But when it comes to the nitty-gritty of deciding or just assessing a dispute or a case study, justice and fairness shatter into pieces.

In order to see where justice lies and whether hard laws can help secure it in some instances, we had to start from the ground up—namely, from the food products and brands, production processes, communities and their practices, and geographies. Most useful and urgent for legal practitioners, scholars, and stakeholders is an inventory of the different issues at stake, rooted in the actual legal cases. An inventory that reflects intellectual challenges emerging from the quotidian role that food plays in our individual lives and that of our families, our communities, and in our institutions. An inventory that can be used as a guide to rethink food IP—to draw comparisons and inspire more fitting ethical, political, and legal principles. And, finally, an inventory that can generate a fruitful dialogue between the different actors in food systems and food markets. This was in keeping with the philosophical approach we endorsed in curating and organizing the disputes and case studies—a variety of pragmatism.

Thus, the book responds to two objectives. First of all, to assemble a diverse portfolio of cases regarding food and IP rights, to take stock of how the use of these rights has evolved and ramified in legal feuds around the globe. This is what the reader will find in the collection of fifty disputes and case studies, which follow this introductory chapter and are organized under eight topics: (I) images; (II) genericity and descriptiveness; (III) language traps; (IV) procedures; (V) menus, recipes, and creativity; (VI) boundaries; (VII) biotech; and (VIII) empowerment. The terrain covered by this sampler is wide-ranging and reaches out to fine-grained aspects of food products, recipes, brands, packaging, and cooking practices. Taken together, the cases bear witness to the importance of the matters at stake, to their complexity and diversity, and to the dangers of reducing a discussion about food and IP to single ethical or legal principles. In fact, while some of the topics treated in the volume have been debated for a long time, many others have never been examined by scholars.

In choosing our disputes and case studies, we aim to display the wealth of conceptual conundrums that pertains to food cultures. But—and this responds to our second objective—we also wanted to organize these disputes and case studies so as to create links with scholarly conversations over issues such as culinary creativity, food justice, food sovereignty, food security, and other pressing matters that pertain to ethical, political, and cultural aspects of food. Accordingly, we showcase such links in three ways. First, for each specific case we review, we provide references (to scholarly research or media coverage, depending on the topic). Second, we present a comprehensive Introduction at the outset of the volume, offering an overview of the questions, issues, and the literature on food and IP rights—that is, a theoretical frame for the interdisciplinary and ever-evolving subject matter. Last, we were lucky enough to have generous colleagues who contributed a foreword and an epilogue to the volume.

The philosophical expertise we employed in the Introduction is essentially theoretical and follows a three-step approach: taking stock of the status quo; devising areas of reflection and negotiation; reassessing and redrawing the status quo. We used philosophy as a tool to tease out the *ontological* and *metaphysical* specificities of the entities at stake, that is, to ascertain their nature and thus offer a bridge between the courtrooms, food items, and human societies. Questions that guided us include: What kinds of entities are we aiming to protect? Which cultural processes do they underpin? Who is responsible for producing them? What is the role of place and environment in determining their identities?

The selection of the 50 case studies was based not only on ontological and metaphysical categories, though; other criteria included geographical location, the typology of legal complaint, and the sort of actors involved. Moreover, we chose the most meaningful and impactful disputes and cases. The systematization we offer also tends to reflect bubbles of scholarly literature and media coverage that often never found their way into the dialogue, to create the potential to bridge conversations and strategies for dealing with the respective issues.

Acknowledgments. We are much indebted to Simona Ovcarike, who helped us compile several of the 50 case studies, and to Friederike Oursin for running a comprehensive and thorough editorial revision of the manuscript. David Forman did not simply write an afterword: he provided substantial feedback on a full draft of the entire manuscript and we are much indebted to him. We are also in debt to our friends and colleagues who provided insights on the matters discussed in this book during quotidian exchanges; we especially thank Andrea Baldini, Nicola Piras, Beatrice Serini, Achille Varzi, and the colleagues at Culinary Mind. Our final and special *grazie* to Min and Rui for their time and support. To Folco, Lelio, and Taka.

Introduction

Food, Philosophy, and Intellectual Property Rights: A Roadmap

If "the linkage between food and intellectual property rights is not obvious" (Srinivas, 2015, p. 381), their relation to theoretical and value-laden issues will be even less transparent to consumers. In this essay we set out to show why it is fruitful—under some respects even urgent—to consider these subjects together, and we offer a roadmap of the questions, issues, and the literature.

1 The Elusive Role of Food-Related Intellectual Property

Intellectual property (IP) contributes to shaping the food domain in many ways. To some extent, its influence is manifest. Most consumers may know that "Champagne" is a term that only some French wine producers may place on the bubbly wines they sell based on strict and historically disputed regulations; and many may be acquainted with the cultural and politico-economical contentions surrounding terms such as "Darjeeling," "Parmesan," or "Tequila." The right to patent genetically modified (GM) crops such as corn, soy, or canola is another topic frequently covered in the news, which tends to divide and polarize public opinion in connection to nutrition and health, enlightened agriculture, and fair markets (Srinivas, 2015; Tansey & Rajotte, 2008).

A large section of food IP, however, never comes to the attention of the international or national media and may escape public scrutiny altogether. These IP rights concern both disputes between industrial food producers as well as those between small local businesses and are the subject of more technical study by legal and paralegal practitioners and industry actors (O'Donnell et al., 2008). Most consumers may not know that Ritter Sport is the only square chocolate bar on the market in many countries due to trademark protection regarding its shape acquired in the 1990s; and many readers have probably never heard of the amusing case of the whale-shaped ice cream cake aptly named Fudgie the Whale, over which shape the American ice cream franchise Carvel owns IP rights. Other IP rights protect the way a food is served; Izzy's Ice Cream Café in Minneapolis, for instance, owns IP rights over Izzy Scoop®, a baby scoop of ice cream placed atop a regular

DOI: 10.4324/9781003433675-1

scoop. IP rights have also been sought and obtained to protect packaging, such as the images that accompany a food product; a notable case we review at the beginning of this book is Queso Manchego v. IQC, where the former was eventually granted exclusive rights by the European Union (EU) to use imagery related to Don Quixote, his horse, and the windmills on the product label. Finally, IP rights have been employed to valorize the creativity of individual chefs running local businesses, like the Cronut, the pastry invented in 2013 by Dominique Ansel, whose dough is reminiscent of a croissant except that it is shaped and fried like a doughnut; or to valorize inventions made with respect to scalable, industrial products, such as the layered technique used by Kevin Hillman to make the first version of the Viennetta ice cream cake in 1982.

As one delves deeper into the matter, it becomes increasingly evident that it is difficult to find a common denominator to all IP rights recognized over food products. They apply to heterogeneous aspects such as shape, brand, serving, process of production, packaging, or the imagery used to accompany the product; and they operate at very different scales. Some food IP rights concern internationally traded products, whose names have come to symbolize a country or a region, like in the case of Chianti, Darjeeling, Rooibos, or Bourbon; while others have effects that are by and large limited to local customers of a single business that owns at best a few shops (such as Dominique Anselm and Izzy Ice Cream) or to a region (such as Carvel, which operates mostly in the Northeast of the United States and in Florida).

Following the numerous food-related IP disputes, court verdicts, and case studies around the globe, we run the risk to lose the forest for the trees. The rationales used to grant IP rights vary wildly and it may be tempting to reach the skeptical conclusion that IP has most often been granted to very specific food items for protecting private business interests (when not vanity) rather than for safeguarding real issues of food justice. After all, no magic ethical golden rule has been put forward to measure, assess, and remedy the justice aspect of those disputes.

We wrote this book because we see an alternative path, which engages philosophical reflection on more empirical grounds and on a case-by-case basis. We believe that IP rights can serve an important role in fostering food justice in contemporary food markets at international, national, and local levels. Indeed, when suitably used, they can directly address issues of linguistic and epistemic justice, besides helping to boost more equitable and transparent trades (see Borghini, 2023, for a recent overview of food justice issues from a philosophical perspective). Obviously, they can also serve to advance less progressive and noble aims, such as promoting the economic interests of individual and already powerful actors. Also, IP rights are not the exclusive legal tools for advancing food justice when it comes to food products, and we shall elaborate on this. Nonetheless, even taking into account their drawbacks and possible alternatives, we believe that IP rights can in some cases be the best (if not the sole) tool for advancing certain socially and culturally meaningful causes.

Thus, the path we follow in this book rejects the skeptical conclusion that no court verdict and no dispute can be ethically assessed; at the same time, it avoids the temptation to impose a top-down, armchair philosophical approach. Our path builds spheres of negotiation from the bottom up, organizing the conversation in ways that bridge it with the rich and textured body of scholarship on food culture, food ethics, and food politics. In the remainder of this Introduction, we elaborate on our approach.

2 Culinary Creativities

IP rights, in their most straightforward and fundamental interpretation, try to protect human inventiveness and creativity as well as the reputations of brands and the interests of consumers in not being confused. To bring evidence in favor of food-related IP, we must, therefore, first take a step back and consider the importance of culinary creativity.

For an individual or a community, the often repetitive and extremely demanding necessities of cooking and preparing food can sometimes be turned into quintessential and primordial forms of creativity, which on special occasions can lead to innovation in lifestyle too. In this role, they are paralleled only by very few other activities, such as singing, dancing, and storytelling or creative use of language. This point has by and large escaped the attention of philosophers working on creativity.[1] For instance, in the contemporary classic anthology edited by Paul and Kaufman (2014), cooking and food are not thematized. And yet, as prominent food journalist Jamila Robinson recently stated in an interview with author Mitchell Davies, "food is the art form that we all participate in."[2]

Culinary creativity can take many forms and have many purposes. It is, arguably, not only for the enjoyment of single individuals, and it is not only linked to private endeavors. And it is not only "practical." Creative components in a cooking process may be very intellectually sophisticated (see, e.g., Gualtieri, 2022), as some contemporary fine dining attests. Also, as philosopher Lisa Heldke (1988) argued, the cooking process can be paralleled to other forms of inquiry, including philosophizing itself. Cooking can be improvisation, as Baldini (2020) discussed. Furthermore, cooking and dining can sometimes be regarded as forms of public art. As Borghini and Baldini (2022) argued, a wide range of culinary practices may be seen as forms of memorial art, social protest art, or art that enhances; these practices do not

---

1 But see Engisch (forthcoming), which shows some avenues to link the philosophical literature on, respectively, creativity and food.
2 *What's Burning*, podcast, Episode 003, January 2022, mins. 11:00–11:04.

include only fine dining. On the contrary, they also distinctively emerge from quotidian gestures in home kitchens or in unpretentious contexts, thus constituting one of the most precious means of creative and artistic expression for neglected and generally disempowered people. Of course, this is not to discount all those who are forced to cook or who must cook to fulfill a social role they did not choose, those who are underpaid for their work or abused in the kitchen. To the contrary, these situations, which by and large are entrenched in the social histories of women and minorities, are even more despicable precisely for the deep-seated role that cooking and preparing food plays in human culture.

In addition, creativity can be studied from the point of view of the places and contexts that give rise to it. Exciting and innovative cooking can take place not only in the setting of a prototypical restaurant, but also in a home setting, in a food trailer, or on the street. The *New York Times* food critic Pete Wells made this claim unapologetically and somewhat controversially by assigning three stars to La Piraña Lechonera in the Bronx, a legendary street food vendor serving Puerto Rican specialties such as *lechón asado*. In other cases, creativity does not rest on what happens in a kitchen (no matter how it is conceived and organized) but on the entire food chain or in a whole food system. A notable example are foods and products that comply with specific, progressive principles, such as animal products that are cruelty-free or Fair Trade products. In these instances, the creative process is due to the agency of some specific people or groups, which took the effort to rethink and reshape the production process. A much older and established way to recognize creativity within food chains and systems rests on emphasizing the *communities* out of which they emerged, which perfected and kept them in existence. This is perhaps the most common way to celebrate the extremely rich variety of recipes and products that humans have invented; they make our lives much more exciting and worth living, if we are lucky enough to be in a position to savor and experience them. The Slow Food Presidia and the Ark of Taste, two repositories promoted by Slow Food we review below, well exemplify the significance and pervasiveness of the culinary creativity related to communities.

Creativity can regard specific aspects too, such as the name given to a food or the logo or image accompanying it. Packaging can be used creatively by food companies to convey messages to consumers, captivate their attention, and eventually convince them to buy a product. Of course, there are limits on the kind of information that can be displayed on packaging. Such content, including brands, cannot mislead consumers as to the characteristics of the product such as geographical provenance, the nature and amount of ingredients, and the quality in general.

Legal disputes are an especially fertile ground for showcasing in what sense cooking and food production in general can be creative, as they force us to consider whether a certain process is unique, if and how it is innovative, who should be credited for its singularity, and so on. A textbook example we included in the selection of the volume (Case 31) concerns the case of Masterpiece Cakeshop v. Colorado Civil Rights Commission. This is one of the very few not strictly IP-related case studies we treat in this volume. However, it deserves to be included as it raises the question of whether a pastry chef can invoke the First Amendment and refuse to make a cake for a specific client—the client in the case being a gay couple—by insisting that their work is a creative act resting on freedom of expression. In a November 16, 2017, *New York Times* article, Adam Liptak wrote about an interview with Floyd Abrams, "the nation's most prominent First Amendment lawyer," which is worth quoting:

> "At first blush, the position of the baker had a good deal of appeal to me," he said. "There was and is no reason to doubt his position was one of conscience, and the visage of state-ordered creation of what could be viewed as some sort of artistic offering certainly set some First Amendment flags flying."

> "But the more I thought about it," Mr. Abrams said, "the more I thought of other possibilities. Could a painter invite the public to his gallery at which he painted portraits of them for a fee but refused to paint black people? Could a musician invite the world to his studio where he wrote songs about them for a fee but refused to do so for Jews or Muslims? The First Amendment protects a lot, but not that conduct."
>
> (Liptak, 2017)

And so, it came about that a culturally salient food item like a wedding cake could serve as fertile ground for reflecting on much broader issues, including the boundaries of what the First Amendment protects.

Now, how was this wealth of culinary creativity (and, ultimately, culture) cushioned from a legal point of view? The contemporary landscape clearly indicates two very distinct, yet often collaborating, strategies: a *soft* one and a *hard* one. IP rights are chief representatives of the latter; but we shall first discuss the former, as an emerging and more fluid form of legal protection.

3 Protecting Culinary Creativity: Soft Legal Tools

The most exploited apparatus within the context of soft legal tools is *cultural heritage* (see Di Giovine and Brulotte (2016) and Lee (2018) for a recent case study). A global initiative in this area that gained traction in recent years is the UNESCO Intangible Cultural Heritage List (Oliveira et al., 2020). It now records among its entries items such as Mexican cuisine, the Mediterranean diet, the French baguette, the gastronomic meal of the French, Japan's

Washoku culture (Cang, 2018), and the art of Neapolitan *"pizzaiuolo"* (Stazio, 2021). Many items are under consideration as we write. As this incomplete list evidences, the items under protection are very different in their nature: We have single types of products (e.g., baguettes), meals, diets, and national culinary cultures. Such diversity risks becoming a drawback when it comes to envisaging forms of protection (Romagnoli, 2019). In fact, it is not entirely clear how much legal force the List has. It is definitely not comparable to a hard legal tool, to be used in court. Specifically, inclusion in the List does not give any actor monopolistic rights over brands or certain manufacturing techniques. Rather, the List functions as a diplomatic and promotional tool, which can be brought forth in political and economic negotiations, especially given the fact that a branch of the United Nations compiled the List (see Parasecoli, 2017).

Besides the UNESCO List, two influential soft legal tools have been promoted by Slow Food—the grassroots organization founded in Italy in 1989—to prevent the disappearance of local food cultures and traditions. In the year 2000, Slow Food began compiling a list of *presidia* (i.e., items that deserve being *protected* against the threat of the loss and decay of the diversity of food practices and cultures) to better emphasize the importance of local food products for the lives of communities and their cultures. As we write, the organization has recognized 645 presidia from 79 countries. The list is rather homogeneous as most of the items are agricultural products, such as specific plant varieties, animal breeds, fermented beverages, honeys, pasta varieties, and so on. Today, Slow Food is a leading global organization, capable of influencing markets and policies on multiple scales. The second initiative is the Ark of Taste, an inventory of "small-scale quality productions that belong to the cultures, history and traditions of the entire planet: an extraordinary heritage of fruits, vegetables, animal breeds, cheeses, breads, sweets and cured meats."[3] To date, the list contains 6024 items from 151 countries. This list, too, contains specific products.[4]

Soft tools flag the importance of a generic product, a specific producer, or a specific product, encouraging consumers and institutions to support its continuous existence. In this sense, their role blurs and merges with the distinctions awarded by independent organizations, including: the Good Food Institute, which issues a yearly list of Good Food Awards; the Rainforest Alliance and the Fair Trade Sustainability Alliance, which curate two independent lists of certified products, based on criteria negotiated and selected according to their ethical value. These lists function as *paralegal tools*, shaping markets, regulating the use of trusted labels, and thus orienting trusting consumers.

Soft legal and paralegal tools play a decisive role in today's food markets—and not only for exclusive or luxury products. A case in point is the

3 See https://www.fondazioneslowfood.com/en/what-we-do/the-ark-of-taste/
4 For a short, slightly dated, but still pertinent commentary on the Slow Food case, see Paxson (2005).

flourishing network of indigenous food producers that has found fertile ground in the tools provided by Slow Food. Dozens of products are recognized either as presidia or are cataloged in the Ark of Taste. In addition, the Indigenous Terra Madre Network (one of Slow Food's networks) hosted a groundbreaking global gathering in 2015 in Shillong (Meghalaya, India), during which over 600 delegates representing indigenous communities, academia, youth, UN agencies and donors from 62 countries participated in three days of conferences addressing the rights of indigenous peoples.[5]

While UNESCO's choice of protecting a wide variety of food items may be seen as questionable, we should note that it also exploits a feature of soft forms of protection: They are especially fitting to flag the cultural importance of loose and vague entities, such as food cultures and diets. It is arguably difficult to enforce issues pertaining to these elusive cultural items in a legal setting. However, when used in soft legal repositories, they can perform more subtle diplomatic functions. The key role of soft tools has been proven especially in the emerging fields of social gastronomy, food diplomacy, and culinary diplomacy. Thanks to the work of dedicated scholars and policymakers such as Paul Rockower (2012, 2020), Johanna Mendelson Forman (2016, 2023), and María Elena García (2021), it is by now standard in numerous social and political settings—ranging from food festivals to government-sponsored programs—to see the food domain as a rich repository of diplomatic and social utensils. These authors provide convincing arguments according to which soft power is frequently the most just forum for seeking protection for a food item, be this a product, a practice, a place, or a space.

Hard tools arguably cannot be employed for this means. It is simply not feasible to imagine hard legal protection for the Mediterranean diet or Mexican cuisine, since they fluidly belong to everyday practices, they inhabit households and other private spaces, and their identity is constantly up for negotiation among multiple actors. We, therefore, cautiously advise and encourage the use of soft legal tools in these circumstances, to remind us of the political importance of certain cultural practices that go beyond products and also look at gastrospaces (Bonotti et al., 2023), food practices, and food ceremonies.

4 Safeguarding Culinary Creativity via Hard Legal Tools: The Case of Geographical Indications

What about hard legal tools? They encompass the enforcement of laws, most especially IP laws, within local, national, and international markets. Hard forms of protection for foods and food products have a long legal history. A global treaty with immense impact (also) on the food sector is the so-called

---

5 See https://www.theindigenouspartnership.org/indigenous-terra-madre

TRIPS Agreement, namely, the Agreement on Trade-Related Aspects of Intellectual Property Rights. The accord was negotiated between the late 1980s and early 1990s, it was signed in 1994, and its enforcement is supervised by the World Trade Organization (WTO) established in 1995. At the time of writing, 164 countries are WTO members. Solicited by Western and industrialized states, the TRIPS Agreement heavily protects IP rights including patents, trademarks, geographical indications (GIs), new plant varieties, and trade secrets. In this agreement, countries such as the United States, the then European Economic Community (now the European Union), and Japan managed to introduce a type of protection similar to, if not identical with, their own IP rules. Among the industries that pushed for the adoption of such a strong IP framework, there were global food, wine, and spirit companies that relied, and still rely, on such a legal framework to recoup investments and make profits. Companies such as Monsanto, for instance, need strong protection of patents and plant variety rights over the genetically modified foodstuff they produce. Likewise, wine, cheese, and ham producers, especially those established in Europe, need protection of exclusive rights over geographical indications such as "Champagne," "Parmigiano," or "Parma Ham." The TRIPS Agreement was also negotiated to please these corporations and the governments lobbied by them.

Against this background, the impact of IP protection in the food domain is not to be underestimated. It is not simply a topic for entertaining guests at a dinner party. IP rights over food products actually influence what we can or cannot purchase and, ultimately, consume; and, furthermore, they—sometimes decisively—influence the diplomatic functions of food products.[6]

IP can determine the fate of a food product and, hence, be of vital importance for food producers, chefs, food traders, and other key actors in food systems. When, in 2008, Italian wine producers of what was once called *Tocai friulano* lost the legal battle against the wine producers from the Tokaj-Hegyalja region of Hungary, their business losses were devastating and changed the course of white wine production in northern Italy's Friuli Venezia Giulia for decades to come.

Yet IP is not just a monopolistic tool aimed at pleasing big companies. It can also enhance the inventiveness of small local actors against the interests of larger corporations, encouraging local interaction within a food system and acting as a countermeasure to the tendency to *scale up* any culinary invention, transforming it into a mass product (see also Broussard, 2007). The Cronut may well never become an industrial product, remaining the specialty of an artisanal shop, produced daily in small quantities, and sold to be consumed within hours. Scaling up production sometimes is a threat to integrity after all.

---

6 See Raimondi et al. (2020) for a study of the economic effects of EU-related GIs in the period 1996–2014.

A fitting example is lard from Colonnata, the very first *presidium* recognized by Slow Food. The recognition generated an unintended boomerang effect: Consumer demand grew and producers tried to increase their output but struggled with preserving the integrity of the product, to the point that Slow Food removed the famous lard from its list of presidia in a move that sparked heated controversy. In addition, and perhaps most importantly, these kinds of recognition, together with IP protection, can be an *empowering tool* for consortia of producers in countries that cannot compete on a par with others in international markets. In this direction, we can indeed list important projects such as the Manual for Geographical Indications in Africa (Bagal et al., 2022) or the initiative that favors the rise of GIs for least developed countries by the United Nations Conference on Trade and Development[7]: Part VIII of this volume contains a selection of important cases that fit this category (an additional case that we could not include but that deserves a mention is that of Goa cashew nuts, which were given GI protection in 2023 by the government of India).

Moreover, by influencing and orienting markets, IP rights shape consumer food choices when shopping, dining out, or simply thinking about what to have for dinner. Hence, they can serve as tools for food sovereignty and food security (see Forsyth & Farran, 2013; Blakeney, 2009; Cullet, 2004). Finally, they can be employed as tools for the preservation of the intangible cultural heritage of certain products, as in the case of GIs.

The leading institution in putting forward laws and regulations to shape and enforce GIs in international markets has been the European Union. This does not come as a surprise as many EU countries such as Italy, France, Spain, Greece, and Portugal are almost unanimously recognized as the home of the most diverse and high-quality food cultures in the world. By way of illustrating the workings of GIs, we now expand on their protection within the EU.

The GI legal regime promoted by the EU primarily focuses on the concept of *terroir*—i.e., roughly, that ecosystem that includes local climatic conditions, geography, topography, and agricultural practices. The term "terroir" is linked to a host of virtues within EU laws that concern the agri-food sector.[8] Indeed, EU GI laws purport to protect not only local producers from those who appropriate and exploit their names in the marketplace: most importantly, they aim to preserve and advance public goods such as agricultural and food biodiversity, cultural heritage and local knowledge, socio-cultural development, and the fight against rural poverty.[9]

---

7 https://unctad.org/topic/least-developed-countries/geographical-indications
8 See, e.g., Belletti and Marescotti (2011); Zappalaglio (2021).
9 See Cullet (2005, pp. 333–336), Zographos (2006), Kono (2009), Gervais (2009), and Dagne (2014) for a discussion of the role that GIs can play in protecting traditional knowledge. For some recent criticism and commentaries, see: Borghini et al. (2023); Bonanno et al. (2020); Gangjee (2017); and Marie-Vivien et al. (2017).

There are currently four pieces of EU legislation on GIs addressing different product categories, i.e., agricultural products and foodstuffs, wines, aromatized wines, and spirit drinks. The first of them—Regulation 2081/92—goes back to the early 1990s and was negotiated in conjunction with the reform of the Common Agricultural Policy. This Regulation harmonized GIs by creating two main titles of protection: the Protected Designations of Origin (PDOs) and the Protected Geographical Indications (PGIs).

The EU firmly protects products with PGIs and PDOs. These titles protect names of products that have qualities linked to the soil and local areas and are made according to specific methods of production (e.g., "Rioja" and "Champagne" wines; "Parmigiano Reggiano" cheese; "Salame Felino;" "Mortadella di Bologna;" "Mutarde de Bougorgne;" and "Gruyère" cheese). PDOs guarantee that the manufacturing process is carried out, in its entirety, in a specific geographical area; to grant a PGI, instead, it is sufficient that one phase of the productive process is performed in the territory in question. Presuming an inextricable link between the quality and reputation of a product and the place of origin, the EU GI system purports to promote cultural and gastronomic heritage.

Under EU law, GIs provide a substantial and wide-ranging protection. They allow GI owners to prevent others from not only exploiting the geographical name (e.g., by misleading consumers as to the geographical origin and quality of the product) but also from making evocative uses of the name, e.g., by accompanying it with expressions such as "kind," "type," "style," "imitation," or the like, or when it is used in translation.[10] Thus, for instance, a German cheese producer cannot use the expressions "Parmigiano-type" or "Parmesan-style" to describe its products, even when it is clear to consumers that the cheese in question is made in Germany and not in the area surrounding the Italian city of Parma. Hence, GI owners are given the right to stop others from exploiting the evocative power of their sign.

Several stakeholders sought to apply the concept of GIs beyond spirits and agricultural products, to include products such as cutlery, leather, ceramics, and glassware (e.g., Murano glass). In fact, a number of EU countries have introduced GI protection for industrial products, and the EU has recently adopted a new regulation on GIs for this category of goods.

The EU provides additional protection for specific foodstuff production methods. This is the so-called Traditional Speciality Guaranteed (TSG). Under EU Regulation 1151/2012, TSG protection does not guarantee that the food comes from a specific geographical area, as PDOs or PGIs do. Rather, it seeks to guarantee that the product be distinctively and specifically traditional in terms of the process of production and ingredients, that is, of "proven

---

10 See, for example, Article 103 of Regulation (EU) No. 1308/2013; Article 13 of Regulation (EU) No. 1151/2012.

usage on the domestic market for a period that allows transmission between generations"—a period of a minimum of thirty years. This Regulation provides the following rationale for the introduction of TSG registration: "to safeguard traditional methods of production and recipes by helping producers of traditional product in marketing and communicating the value-adding attributes of their traditional recipes and products to consumers." An iconic product to have obtained the TSG title in the EU is Pizza Napoletana—a title that is owned and managed by the Associazione Vera Pizza Napoletana. Consequently, this association could take legal action against anyone in the EU who sells pizza and uses the term "Pizza Napoletana" without following the prescribed traditional manufacturing technique (see Stazio, 2021, for an analysis of the cultural aspects of TSG granting). All TSG owners would in theory be able to enforce what is effectively a monopolistic right over a specific food brand against competitors who use it without respecting the traditional production process. We used the words "in theory" as to the best of our knowledge there is no TSG-related case law yet, which seems to suggest that this kind of protection offered by the EU is more theoretical than practical.

This long discussion of GIs within the EU attests to the intricacies of their legal status and to the complex negotiations they have solicited and still solicit. While the EU's understanding of GIs exercises a major influence on international markets, serving also as a template for GIs in emerging markets (see, e.g., the cases of Madd de Casamance in Senegal or Cabrito de Tete in Mozambique, highlighted in this volume), other countries have a different approach to GIs. Most notably, in the United States GIs are protected, quite unlike in the EU, as a sub-category of trademarks; therefore they are not linked in essence to geographical regions, terroir, traditions, and so on. In the words of legal scholar Michael Roberts:

> [i]n the United States, on the contrary, GIs are a subset of trademarks and protected through certification marks. GIs serve the same functions as trademarks because like trademarks they are source-identifiers, guarantees of quality, and valuable business interests. Certification marks are owned by private certifying organizations, which license their use to other entities (i.e., the owning organization cannot itself use the mark). The certifier is responsible for submitting an application to the US Patent and Trademark Office (USPTO) and auditing the practices of users of the mark to ensure compliance with the certification mark's standards.
>
> (Roberts, 2016, p. 285).

The differences in GI regimes for food products between the EU and the United States stand as a mark of the often tense conversations that surround their enforcement. If we cannot even converge on a common regime, how can we hope to agree on the details of the laws and regulations, not to mention on specific court rulings? Maybe we should do away with IP in the food domain?

5 Criticisms

IP overprotection has been criticized by both scholars and citizens at large (May & Sell, 2005). So much so that, for instance, a global network of political parties—called "pirate parties"—has made it its chief goal to abolish most copyright protections. Drawing from the general literature criticizing or at least downplaying IP rights, we can devise three lines of argument that apply to food IP too.

The first line of argument rests on the idea that IP rights are not an ethical means to protect human genius and creativity; rather, they favor the monopolistic interests of few actors (Boldrin & Levin, 2009). While we praise the fact that IP rights often aim at encouraging creativity and inventiveness (see, e.g., the Lost Spirits patents covering a revolutionary method of producing mature rum and whiskey within days, treated in this book), we also want to point out that IP may be used in a way that is arguably contrary to the promotion of public interests. The recent heated debate around patenting Covid-19 vaccines and the high prices that these IP rights often impose, especially in developing countries, stand testament to that. Similarly, one may also mention the overprotection of copyright, which—in some circumstances—may limit access to culture and information as well as discourage follow-on and downstream creativity. These lines of argument may even be stronger in the case of food, which is ubiquitous and enters even the most intimate aspects of our lives— our homes, our most special moments, our most humbling situations (e.g., in a hospital bed), and our most basic forms of existence (e.g., infant formula).

The second line of argument arises out of a widespread suspicion, namely, that food IP does not sustain culinary creativity, but that it is rather the outgrowth of a different and despicable human instinct: dominion over and elimination of competitors. Thus, IP protection would primarily or solely serve the purposes of individual actors (e.g., chefs and shopkeepers), companies, and consortia (e.g., those of Champagne, Porto, or Parmigiano), ultimately driven by the desire to monopolize the market and edge out competitors (see Haugen, 2014; Oguamanam, 2006). In this sense, this line of argument stands in opposition to the protection of food heritage, as argued for instance in the case of Serrano cheese from Rio Grande do Sul, Brazil. In this case, qualitative research has analyzed the role of GIs in conserving the cultural identity of the cheese and found that instead of protecting and preserving the local culinary heritage, GI rules are likely to produce standardized manufacturing methods (Vitrolles, 2011).

Granted, both lines of argument deserve closer scrutiny and discussion. Simplifying a perhaps longer conversation, we shall then note that, while these lines have some merit, they also seem to discount the fact that food IP has served and can still serve to regulate market struggles. IP policies are, in fact, the most widespread and perhaps the most intuitive legal tool to regulate markets at all levels from an institutional point of view. But this is not to say, of course, that food IP is perfect as it is, as we shall discuss momentarily.

The third argument is, more exactly, an attitude. It sees food IP, especially when it comes to recipes created by chefs, as a *negative space*. The trend in the kitchen is not to use legal means to defend one's own culinary creations but to use social norms as well as multiple channels of communication to show disappointment (Raustiala & Sprigman, 2012). After all, as the US government itself notes, "if you have secret ingredients to a recipe that you do not wish to be revealed, you should not submit your recipe for registration, because applications and deposit copies are public records."[11] Thus, the place for debating and negotiating food identities is the media, social media, and the public sphere of communication in general.

This argument is very radical and, we think, too optimistic with respect to the capacities of human societies to solve their issues through fair and transparent communication. Not all food actors have the same powers when it comes to communication. The risk is simply that those actors aggressively investing in "stealing ideas" while protecting their image through widespread campaigns and advertisements could dominate the market. In fact, in most countries there are slim chances of blocking the stealing of recipes by recurring to hard legal tools.[12] This, without doubt, seems unfair.

The third argument implicitly raises some important questions regarding the legitimate limitation of IP rights. How far should such legal means extend in space and time? Should they enter our home kitchens, too, or only certain sorts of public venues? Should they hold only for for-profit establishments? Should they hold for a very limited number of years? What about specific items, such as taste? In this sense, one may well argue that certain IP rights, such as GIs, are at a crossroads: Their legal and civic value will not be able to stand the challenges that climatic, societal, and economic changes will bring about (Calboli & Ng Loy, 2017).[13]

A fourth and final line of argument suggests a *deflationary attitude* toward food IP. In brief, even if we agree that IP can have a positive impact on food systems and food cultures, such impact could equally be achieved via the employment of soft legal tools. Yet, the latter are far less complex and controversial than the former. In fact, hard tools are too often employed selectively and without a broad consultation with all the relevant stakeholders, while this is not the case with soft legal tools, which can more easily adapt to and reflect stakeholders' perspectives. Hence, we should prefer soft to hard legal tools.

11 See https://www.copyright.gov/help/faq/faq-protect.html
12 For example, in the United States: "A mere listing of ingredients or contents, or a simple set of directions, is uncopyrightable. As a result, the Office cannot register recipes consisting of a set of ingredients and a process for preparing a dish. In contrast, a recipe that creatively explains or depicts how or why to perform a particular activity may be copyrightable" (see Circular 33, Works Not Protected by Copyright: https://www.copyright.gov/circs/circ33.pdf).
13 See https://www.reuters.com/article/us-eu-copyright-netherlands-food-idUSKCN1NI1IN

GIs offer a neat case in point here. There is great confusion regarding what they are and why they should even exist, with a suspicion that they may be there to protect monopolistic interests; and we have argued elsewhere that they may be rethought to encompass different tasks and to more suitably protect community and individual values. Indeed, while we praise the important function GIs have in terms of promoting the intangible cultural heritage related to food production (see, e.g., the cases concerning South Africa's Red Bush tea (Case 44) and Benin's Sugarloaf pineapple (Case 47)), we also cannot help but highlight certain excesses such protection sometimes produces. We refer here, for example, to two cheese-related disputes decided by the Court of Justice of the European Union (CJEU) that will be analyzed in this book, namely the Queso Manchego and Morbier cases. As we will see, these two CJEU decisions seem to go too far. As a matter of fact, one may argue that granting a monopoly on the shape or form of a product (as happened in Morbier) as well as certain imagery, which merely evokes characters and landscapes of the geographical area related to a specific GI (as occurred with Queso Manchego), is inherently contrary to free trade and competition principles.

On the other hand, we welcome the CJEU decision in Levola Hengelo v. Smilde Foods[14] where a cheese producer took a copyright-based legal action against a competitor because they claimed their product tasted the same as theirs. The top EU court held that, in addition to constituting an author's original expression, a work is copyrightable if it is "expressed in a manner which makes it identifiable with sufficient precision and objectivity, even though that expression is not necessarily in permanent form." The CJEU is basically telling us here that we cannot give copyright protection to something which is vague and subjective—and cheese tastes are exactly this. As mentioned, this is certainly the right decision since providing cheese tastes with copyright protection would certainly overstretch the boundaries of copyrightable subject matter.

This fourth line of argument against food IP has a different spin: Unlike the first three lines of argument, it does not call for the abolition or major softening of all food IP rights, as it agrees that they cannot be completely replaced by soft legal and paralegal tools. Rather, it asks for a rethinking of when to employ food IP and in which form. The call is for more inclusive tools, which are in sight today also thanks to a wide array of methods such as mini-publics and citizen science, that can represent the perspectives and needs of a wider spectrum of stakeholders (see Borghini et al., 2023).

---

14 See https://eur-lex.europa.eu/legal-content/GA/TXT/?uri=CELEX:62017CN0310

6 Philosophical Guidance

Let us take stock. We have seen how varied and fine-grained the field of items and practices is that may suitably fall under the scope of soft and hard legal tools in the food domain. We have also provided an overview of the intricacies and divergences in applying IP rights to food items. Finally, we have reviewed four lines of criticism against the application of such rights to foodstuff. And yet, we have reached some sort of impasse. By itself, the status quo does not provide enough evidence to rule in favor or against IP in the food domain. In fact, as we shall now move to suggest, the guidance needed does not concern *whether* IP rights can be applied to such a domain—they obviously can—but *when* they should be applied, namely, based on which specific rationale. This is where philosophy should come to the rescue: in providing a map of the issues at stake, and in devising shared areas of negotiation and discussion.

Now, the philosophical guidance we bring into play in our analysis calls for some contextualization, as it is rooted in recent scholarship in the philosophy of food. According to a standard approach, a philosophical contribution to an issue should seek out general answers to general questions, e.g., by providing general principles. Thus, for instance, when confronted with questions of justice, philosophy can contribute general justice principles, such as the utilitarian rule according to which—roughly—one ought always to choose the course of action that produces the greatest good for the greatest number of people. But, when calculating the utility function of granting (or not granting) an IP right to a given food item, how are we supposed to weigh according to single scale factors as heterogeneous as community values, individual claims, environmental and geographic data?

A lesson we can draw from the numerous forms and instances of creativity we cited is that in order to adequately capture the questions and issues at stake, we need to delve into the nature of the entities and practices under consideration. Is it a food product at stake? Or is it a more subtle aspect, such as a quality of the product or a part of the production process? If a method of consumption is at stake, how should we approach the matter? What if the case concerns an entire food chain or food system, or even an entire culture? To raise these sorts of interrogatives is to take an *ontological* and a *metaphysical* perspective on the food world, with a pragmatic inclination.

Food provides a fertile ground to exercise a pragmatist approach to theoretical and value-laden questions. Thus, for instance, we could wonder what a recipe is and what determines the identity of a recipe (Borghini, 2015; Borghini & Engisch, 2022); or we could delve into specific kinds of recipes, such as historical recipes (Korsmeyer 2022). We could employ such an approach to investigate food labels too, such as *authentic* (Strohl, 2019), *local* (Borghini et al., 2022), or *natural* (Siipi, 2013). Indeed, the preparatory ground for this study of food, philosophy, and IP was a conference devoted primarily to the ontology and metaphysics of recipes, together with the subsequent anthology on the philosophy of recipes edited by Borghini and Engisch (2022), which includes an essay by Bonadio and Weissenberger (2022) that surveys the extant literature and cases for claiming IP rights over food presentations and recipes.

To date, no study takes stock of the different typologies and issues at stake when it comes to IP in the food domain. The philosophical guidance we put to use was in organizing the materials so as to create the conditions for a constructive and positive dialogue among different actors, including scholars from different fields that seldom talk to each other. More specifically, the theoretical approach we have adopted in organizing the fifty cases contained in this volume can be schematized in the following three steps.

Step 1. During the first step, we *took stock* of the extant literature and case studies. We amassed a large number of cases and surveyed the diverse array of scholarly studies covering IP in the food domain.

Step 2. In a subsequent phase, we sorted out key *areas of case studies.* These are essentially the eight categories under which the cases in the volume are arranged. Focusing on the entities at stake, we tried to tease out abstract categories that can build bridges among legal practice, the ways in which non-legal scholars discuss food items and food cultures, and the perspectives of lay consumers. Here below are the eight categories that emerged as most salient, along with a brief description of each one. This is not to say, of course, that additional categories may not be discerned and added in the future. Also, some cases would comfortably sit in more than one area; however, we decided to categorize each study only within one of the eight groups for, let us call them, "administrative" purposes.

1) *Images.* To think of food solely in terms of its biochemical properties is unreasonably reductive. An intuitive and immediate way to support this claim is by pointing out the importance that food representation has in food markets and systems. Consumers do not buy biochemical items, they buy narratives, which are mediated by language and images. In this section we focus on a series of classic disputes that concern the image of a food, be it the shape of the product itself (e.g., Ritter Sport chocolate bars), the shape of its package (e.g., Oatly), or the image accompanying the product (e.g., Queso Manchego).

2) *Genericity and Descriptiveness.* Language is a primary medium for food representation—but whose language matters more and most? In this section we collect classic and significant disputes that concerned whether a certain term was generically picking out some foodstuff or, rather, whether producers who operate in specific geographical locations have an exclusive right to utilize a term. The list includes "feta," "parmesan," "champagne," "tequila," and "mānuka."

3) *Language Traps.* Language can be seen as a trap, too, misguiding consumers in attributing characteristics to a product that, in fact, it does not possess. Here, IP can come to the rescue of the misappropriation of specific linguistic means to correctly portray a product to consumers. However, the cases we review also show how IP can be employed by more powerful actors to impede local producers from using certain terms.

4) *Procedures.* Identity is often tied to procedures; think of the difference that modifiers such as "artisanal" or "organic" can make to the perception of a food product. Whenever new techniques and technologies of production are introduced, the question arises of whether identity is preserved. In this section we cluster cases that seemed to substantially alter the identity of a product to some, but not to others. The list includes chemical aging, packaging, durability, cooking technique (battering), fermentation, and smuggling.

5) *Menus, Recipes, and Creativity.* Cooking and producing food are first and foremost a creative process. Sometimes, IP can be a powerful tool to reward the innovation brought about by some local actors (a single cook or chef, or the effort of a kitchen or group), especially against exploitative attempts by economically more powerful actors to appropriate the food and scale up its production. Legal cases in this area have yet to involve particularly poignant situations, such as those involving cultural appropriation of indigenous communities; however, the cases we review could be applied to those situations too. Another poignant issue related to creativity emerged with the wedding cake dispute, where the act of delivering a wedding cake was used to assess whether a pastry chef could refuse to make a cake based on the fact that their services are creative by nature.

6) *Boundaries.* The identity of food products can develop in agreement or in contrast with geographical and political boundaries. Products or people can cross boundaries or can develop specificities because such boundaries exist. The cases clustered under this topic are rooted in divergent perspectives over the roles assigned to some boundaries. We selected a spectrum of studies from different world regions: India v. Pakistan; Peru v. Chile; Australia v. New Zealand; Malaysia v. Indonesia; Korea v. China; Spain v. Argentina; Czech Republic v. United States of America.

7) *Biotech.* Food IP does not always concern historically rich items. Some of the foods are novel to a certain group of consumers or novel in general, that is, they have been freshly invented by researchers. Whether such innovations should be rewarded with IP protection or not can be disputed. Cases we review in this section had a remarkable impact on public opinion as well as on markets and institutions. They include two disputes involving Monsanto over plants produced from GM seeds; two cases of patent protection in Europe for products obtained from

essentially biological processes; and the more recent patent dispute over heme (a key ingredient for producing meat substitutes).

8) *Empowerment.* In the last section we collect cases where IP is utilized to empower consortia from less economically and politically competitive countries, in order to distinguish and boost their specialty products. The list includes South Africa's Red Bush tea, Senegal's Madd de Casamance, Mozambique's Cabrito de Tete, Benin's Sugarloaf pineapple, Jamaica's Beef Jerk and Demerara Rum, and Café de Colombia.

Step 3. Rethinking. The curated collection we put together shows how rich the terrain is for IP in the food domain. Most importantly, the collection should be used as a means to showcase the asymmetries that actors face when resorting to the hard legal tool of IP to protect their interests. The third step of the theoretical framework that guided us, therefore, consists of a process of re-envisaging solutions for the questions at stake, e.g., how should we rethink GIs in light of climate change? (See, on this specific example, Borghini et al., 2023.) IP rights have been used inside and outside of courtrooms often by powerful economic and political actors: larger international corporations; richer governments with more persuasive means on the international scene; local chefs and shops with arguably easier access to legal avenues. In what ways can we promote more equitable means to access legal services to enforce food IP for more fragile actors, i.e., those living as minorities in their regions, or operating in countries that cannot offer adequate support?

Implicitly, the curated collection of fifty cases that we offer here may give indications as to how to answer (some of) these questions and their cognates. To address them in full, however, would require a type of exercise that would not be germane to this volume. In fact, many of the questions we unearth await being transcribed and considered by a wide audience. They sit at the intersection between the obscure work of bureaucrats and justice courts and the dense papers of philosophers. In addition, as we write, there are a host of new issues with food IP appearing on the horizon, which we address in the final section of the volume.

References

Bagal, M., Vittori, M., & Samper, L. F. (2022). *Manual for geographical indications in Africa.* European Union Intellectual Property Office.

Baldini, A. (2020). Signature (and) dishes. *Humana. Mente – Journal of Philosophical Studies, 13*(38), 83–110.

Belletti, G., & Marescotti, A. (2011). Origin products, geographical indications and rural development. In E. Barham & B. Sylvander (Eds.), *Labels of origin for food: Local development, global recognition* (pp. 75–91). CAB International.

Blakeney, M. (2009). *Intellectual property rights and food security.* Cabi.

Boldrin, M., & Levine, D. K. (2008). *Against intellectual monopoly*. Cambridge University Press.

Bonadio, E., & Weissenberger, N. (2022). Food presentations and recipes: Is there a space for copyright and other intellectual property rights? In A. Borghini & P. Engisch (Eds.), *A philosophy of recipes: Making, experiencing, and valuing* (pp. 199–214). Bloomsbury.

Bonanno, A., Sekine, K., & Feuer, H. N. (Eds.). (2020). *Geographical indication and global agri-food: Development and democratization*. Routledge.

Bonotti, M., Borghini, A., Piras, N., & Serini, B. (2023). The justice and ontology of gastrospaces. *Ethical Theory and Moral Practice, 26*(1), 91–111.

Borghini, A. (2023). Food justice. In M. Sellers & S. Kirste (Eds.). *Encyclopedia of the philosophy of law and social philosophy*. Springer. https://doi.org/10.1007/978-94 -007-6730-0_1026-1

Borghini, A., & Baldini, A. (2022). Cooking and dining as forms of public art. *Food, Culture & Society, 25*(2), 310–327.

Borghini, A., & Engisch, P. (Eds.). (2022). *A philosophy of recipes: Making, experiencing, and valuing*. Bloomsbury.

Borghini, A., Piras, N., & Serini, B. (2023). Hot grapes: How to locally redesign geographical indications to address the impact of climate change. *World Development Sustainability, 2*, Article 100043.

Broussard, J. A. (2007). An intellectual property food fight: Why copyright law should embrace culinary innovation. *Vanderbilt Journal of Entertainment and Technology Law, 10*(3), 691–699.

Calboli, I., & Ng-Loy, W. L. (Eds.). (2017). *Geographical indications at the crossroads of trade, development, and culture: Focus on Asia-Pacific*. Cambridge University Press.

Cang, V. (2018). Japan's Washoku as intangible heritage: The role of national food traditions in UNESCO's cultural heritage scheme. *International Journal of Cultural Property, 25*(4), 491–513.

Cullet, P. (2004). *Food security and intellectual property rights in developing countries*. RIBios (Réseau interdisciplinaire biosécurité): Institut universitaire d'études du développement (IUED)..

Cullet, P. (2005). *Intellectual property protection and sustainable development*. LexisNexis Butterworths.

Dagne, T. W. (2014). *Intellectual property and traditional knowledge in the global economy: Translating geographical indications for development*. Routledge.

Di Giovine, M. A., & Brulotte, R. L. (2016). Introduction: Food and foodways as cultural heritage. In R. L. Brulotte & M. A. Di Giovine (Eds.), *Edible identities: Food as cultural heritage* (pp. 1–27). Routledge.

Engisch, P. (forthcoming). Creativity, imagination, and the culinary arts. In A. Kind & J. Langkau (Eds.), *Oxford handbook of creativity, imagination, and the subject*. Oxford University Press.

Forman, J. M. (2016). *Foreign policy in the kitchen*. E-International Relations. https:// www.e-ir.info/pdf/66045

Forman, J. M., & LeJeune, K. (2023). Elevating gastrodiplomacy's role in marketing identity. In F. Fusté-Forné & E. Wolf (Eds.), *Contemporary advances in food tourism management and marketing* (pp. 199–211). Taylor and Francis.

Forsyth, M., & Farran, S. (2013). Intellectual property and food security in least developed countries. *Third World Quarterly, 34*(3), 516–533.

Gangjee, D. S. (2017). Proving provenance? Geographical indications certification and its ambiguities. *World Development, 98*, 12–24.

Gervais, D. (2009). Traditional knowledge: Are we closer to the answers? The potential role of geographical indications. *ILSA Journal of International and Comperative Law, 15*(2), 551–567.

Gualtieri, G. (2022). Is cuisine art? Considering art and craft as conceptual categories in American fine dining. *Poetics, 95*, Article 101705.

Haugen, H. M. (2014). The right to food, farmers' rights and intellectual property rights: Can competing law be reconciled? In N. C. S. Lambek, P. Claeys, A. Wong, & L. Brilmayer (Eds.), *Rethinking food systems: structural challenges, new strategies and the law* (pp. 195–218). Springer.

Heldke, L. (1988). Recipes for theory making. *Hypatia, 3*(2), 15–29. Reprinted in Borghini & Engisch (2022), pp. 173–184.

Kono, T. (2009). Geographical indication and intangible cultural heritage. In B. Ubertazzi & E. Muñiz Espada (Eds.), *Le Indicazioni di Qualità degli Alimenti. Diritto internazionale ed europeo* (pp. 289–293). Giuffrè Editore.

Korsmeyer, C. (2022). Historical dishes and the search for past tastes. In A. Borghini & P. Engisch (Eds.), *A philosophy of recipes: Making, experiencing, and valuing* (pp. 99–110). Bloomsbury.

Lee, G. (2018). How to protect traditional food and foodways effectively in terms of intangible cultural heritage and intellectual property laws in the republic of Korea. *International Journal of Cultural Property, 25*(4), 543–572.

Liptak, A. (2017, November 6, 2017). Where to draw line on free speech? Wedding cake case vexes lawyers. *The New York Times.* https://www.nytimes.com/2017/11/06/us/politics/gay-wedding-cake-free-speech-first-amendment-supreme-court.html

Marie-Vivien, D., Bérard, L., Boutonnet, J. P., & Casabianca, F. (2017). Are French geographical indications losing their soul? Analyzing recent developments in the governance of the link to the origin in France. *World Development, 98*, 25–34.

May, C., & Sell, S. K. (Eds.). (2005). *Intellectual property rights: A critical history.* Lynne Rienner.

O'Donnell, R. W., O'Malley, J. J., Huis, R. J., & Halt, G. B. (2008). *Intellectual property in the food technology industry: Protecting your innovation.* Springer Science & Business Media.

Oguamanam, C. (2006). Intellectual property rights in plant genetic resources: Farmers' rights and food security of indigenous and local communities. *Drake Journal of Agricultural Law, 11*, 273–305.

Oliveira, B. S., Tricárico, L. T., Sohn, A. P. L., & Pontes, N. (2020). The culinary intangible cultural heritage of UNESCO: A review of journal articles in EBSCO platform. *Journal of Culinary Science & Technology, 18*(2), 138–156.

Parasecoli, F. (2017). *Knowing where it comes from: Labeling traditional foods to compete in a global market.* University of Iowa Press.

Paul, E. S., & Kaufman, S. B. (Eds.). (2014). *The philosophy of creativity: New essays.* Oxford University Press.

Paxson, H. (2005). Slow food in a fat society: Satisfying ethical appetites. *Gastronomica, 5*(1), 14–18.

Raimondi, V., Falco, C., Curzi, D., & Olper, A. (2020). Trade effects of geographical indication policy: The EU case. *Journal of Agricultural Economics, 71*(2), 330–356.

Raustiala, K., & Sprigman C. J. (2012). *The knockoff economy: How imitation sparks innovation*. Oxford University Press.

Rockower, P. S. (2012). Recipes for gastrodiplomacy. *Place Branding and Public Diplomacy, 8*(3), 235–246.

Rockower, P. S. (2020). A guide to gastrodiplomacy. In N. Snow & N. J. Cull (Eds.), *Routledge handbook of public diplomacy* (pp. 205–212). Routledge.

Romagnoli, M. (2019). Gastronomic heritage elements at UNESCO: Problems, reflections on and interpretations of a new heritage category. *International Journal of Intangible Heritage, 14*, 158–171.

Siipi, H. (2013). Is natural food healthy? *Journal of Agricultural and Environmental Ethics, 26*(4), 797–812.

Srinivas, K. R. (2015). Intellectual property rights and the politics of food. In R. J. Herring (Ed.), *The Oxford handbook of food, politics, and society* (pp. 381–406). Oxford University Press.

Stazio, M. (2021). Verace glocal pizza. Localized globalism and globalized localism in the Neapolitan artisan pizza. *Food, Culture & Society, 24*(3), 406–430.

Strohl, M. (2019). On culinary authenticity: Strohl on culinary authenticity. *The Journal of Aesthetics and Art Criticism, 77*(2), 157–167.

Tansey, G., & Rajotte, T. (Eds.). (2008). *The future control of food: A guide to international negotiations and rules on intellectual property, biodiversity and food security*. Earthscan.

Vitrolles, D. (2011). When geographical indication conflicts with food heritage protection. The case of Serrano cheese from Rio Grande do Sul, Brazil. *Anthropology of Food, 8*. https://doi.org/10.4000/aof.6809

Zappalaglio, A. (2021). *The transformation of EU geographical indications law: The present, past and future of the origin link*. Routledge.

Zographos, D. (2006). Can geographical indications be a viable alternative for the protection of traditional cultural expressions? In F. Macmillan & K. Bowrey (Eds.), *New directions in copyright law* (pp. 37–55). Edward Elgar.

Part I

Images

1   Imagery

Queso Manchego v. IQC

Queso Manchego is a kind of pressed cheese produced from sheep's milk in the Castilla La Mancha region of Spain by following a traditional production technique. Made from pasteurized milk, it needs a maturation period of 30 days for cheeses weighing less than or equal to 1.5 kg, and from 60 days up to a maximum of 2 years for larger cheeses. It is manufactured in four provinces of Castilla La Mancha, namely Toledo, Cuenca, Albacete, and Ciudad Real. In June 1996, this Spanish cheese obtained European Union Protected Designation of Origin (PDO) status.

According to PDO specifications:

> the geographical area of La Mancha is located in the southern part of the central plateau of the peninsula and is characterised by a low relief descending to the Atlantic. La Mancha is a high plain with lime-clay soils and its pastureland has lime- and loam-rich substrates. The area has an extreme climate and experiences wide variations characteristic of a continental climate, with very cold winters and hot summers. The temperature occasionally reaches 40 °C, sometimes varying by 20 °C over the course of a day and 50 °C over the year. Precipitation is scant, making the region one of the more arid areas of Spain, its extremely dry environment having a relative humidity of around 65 %. … The area's soil and climatic conditions have had a great influence on the processes of natural selection that have made the Manchega breed of sheep the breed best adapted to the area and producing a milk that gives "Queso Manchego" its characteristic colour, aroma, flavour and texture.

During the 2010s, the Queso Manchego PDO was at the center of a landmark dispute, which concerned the role of images in representing a geographical indication: on one side, the Queso Manchego Foundation, which manages and protects this PDO, and on the other side Industrial Quesera Cuquerella SL (IQC), a well-known cheese producer also based in the Mancha region.

The IQC produced cheeses not covered by PDO specifications and used certain signs and names, including landscapes and images typical of

DOI: 10.4324/9781003433675-3

La Mancha, which were alleged to be "evocative" of the PDO in question. Specifically, the IQC sold cheese with packaging showing imagery linked to Don Quixote—a popular literary character created by the Spanish writer Cervantes—including windmills and sheep. Windmills are a popular sight in the La Mancha landscape (in Cervantes' novel, Don Quixote famously battled windmills). Additionally, as the Court of Justice of the European Union (CJEU) noted in its ruling, one of the IQC's cheese names is "Rocinante," which is also the name of Don Quixote de La Mancha's horse as narrated by Cervantes.

Initially dismissed by the Audiencia Provincial de Albacete (Provincial Court, Albacete, Spain) in 2014, the case was then referred to the CJEU by the Spanish Supreme Court which asked for clarifications on the scope of protection conferred by PDOs against the evocation of the geographical name.

Then, in 2019, the CJEU found that the imagery used by the IQC on the packaging of its cheese amounted to an unlawful evocation of the PDO. The CJEU clarified that geographical indication protection is given against "any evocation" of the term, and that—added the court—what counts is whether a word or a figurative element can remind consumers of the image of the product protected by the geographical designation.

This finding has clearly broadened the scope of protection available to the holders of PDOs beyond the use of visually or phonetically similar names, following a 1999 ruling over the protection of Gorgonzola cheese and a 2018 ruling concerning the protection of Scotch whisky. It is certainly an extension of the scope of rights originally offered by PDOs—an extension which has however been criticized by several commentators. The CJEU also confirmed that, even if a product was manufactured in the geographical area in question, it must still be considered an infringement if it does not comply with the requirements mentioned in the PDO specification.

Sources

Capelli, F., & Klaus, B. (2019). Protection of geographic indications and designations of origin in the Queso Manchego Case. *European Food and Feed Law Review*, *14*(5), 453–458.

Court of Justice EU, March 4, 1999, Consorzio per la tutela del formaggio Gorgonzola, C-87/97.

Court of Justice EU, June 7, 2018, Scotch Whisky Association, C-44/17.

Court of Justice EU, May 2, 2019, Fundación Queso Manchego v. IQC, C-614/17.

2   Visual Appearance
Morbier v. Société Fromagère du Livradois

Morbier is a semi-soft cow's milk cheese which takes its name from the small village of Morbier in the Jura department in Bourgogne-Franche-Comté in eastern France. In the European Union, the cheese has been protected by a Protected Designation of Origin (PDO) since 2000. It is characterized by a black line that horizontally divides the wheel into two halves. The line was originally made of cinder, but it is now made of vegetable carbon, which is also mentioned by the PDO specification as an ingredient. The black line traces back to the nineteenth century when producers would put curd into a round mold, add the vegetable carbon, and mix it with cow's milk. According to PDO specifications:

> [t]he shape of the cheese (a medium-sized cylinder) was originally adapted to production on mountain farms. Dual production, corresponding to two milkings, makes it possible to obtain quite a large size, limiting losses during storage. This size will subsequently be taken over by the cheese dairies (cheesemaking cooperatives), thereby enabling cheese production when the level of milk production is low. This link with the making of cooked pressed pastes, and in particular "Comté," is found in the rind smearing techniques. This type of care contributes, beyond appearance, to the special taste of the cheese. Using wood for maturing constitutes a direct link with the technological requirements and with the existence nearby of large coniferous forests which are part of the natural environment. [...] The central black line was initially obtained by using soot from the cauldron. This technique affirms the link with the production of cooked pressed pastes in Franche-Comté.

Since 1979, the Société Fromagère du Livradois has been producing the same cheese, but because the cheese was not produced within the geographical area reserved for Morbier cheese, it was sold under the name "Montboissié du Haut Livradois."

In 2013 the Syndicat interprofessionnel de défense du fromage Morbier commenced legal proceedings against the Société Fromagère du Livradois,

DOI: 10.4324/9781003433675-4

arguing that their cheese had the same visual appearance as Morbier's. Morbier claimed that the Société was engaging in parasitic and unfair competition practices by producing and marketing a cheese with a similar shape and appearance. This would allow the Société Fromagère du Livradois to mislead consumers as to the trade source of the cheese as well as to take unfair advantage of the celebrity of Morbier's cheese. Such claims, however, were initially dismissed by the French courts, by clarifying that the PDO is only intended to protect a product's name and not its appearance, shape, or features.

The case was eventually referred to the Court of Justice of the European Union (CJEU). In 2020, the top European court ruled that the imitation not only of the protected geographical name, but also of the visual appearance of a PDO product constitutes a geographical indication infringement if the characterizing feature is reproduced so as to possibly confuse consumers as to who produces and sells the good itself. According to the CJEU press release following its decision:

> the possibility remains that the reproduction of the shape or appearance of a product may be a PDO infringement without that name appearing either on the product in question or on its packaging. This will be the case where that reproduction is liable to mislead the consumer as to the true origin of the product in question. In order to determine whether that is the case, it is necessary, in particular, to assess whether an element of the appearance of the product covered by the registered name constitutes a baseline characteristic which is particularly distinctive of that product so that its reproduction may, in conjunction with all the relevant factors in the case in point, lead the consumer to believe that the product containing that reproduction is a product covered by that registered name.

Sources

Court of Justice EU, Syndicat interprofessionnel de défense du fromage Morbier v. Société Fromagère du Livradois SAS, December 17, 2020, C-783/19.

3 Shape and Packaging
Ferrero Rocher v. Ruchi International

Ferrero is a well-known Italian manufacturer of chocolate and confectionery products that was founded in 1946 and is now the world's fourth largest confectionery producer. The company is well known for producing and selling the iconic Ferrero Rocher, a chocolate confectionery with "contrasting layers: a whole crunchy hazelnut in the heart, a delicious creamy hazelnut filling, a crisp wafer shell covered with chocolate and gently roasted hazelnut pieces."[1] Ferrero has been keen to protect this very distinctive trade dress in many countries around the world, together with its registered trademark.

In 2012, Ferrero launched a legal action in India against the manufacturer of chocolate products named Golden Passion and its Indian distributor Ruchi International. The chocolates' shape and packaging were indeed a lookalike of Ferrero Rocher. The Italian company claimed that the peculiar shape of its famous chocolates enjoys significant goodwill and a long-standing reputation in many countries around the world including India.

In 2018, the High Court of Delhi decided the case, first acknowledging the fame acquired by Ferrero Rocher's iconic trade dress. Specifically, it noted that the Italian company had demonstrated that such dress has

acquired the status of "well-known mark" by virtue of various factors such as use of its trade mark and trade dress since as long back as 1982 and its subsequent registration, its widespread business across numerous countries, the immense goodwill and reputation acquired by it around the world, the wide scale advertising and promotional activities carried out by plaintiff and its massive turnover on annual basis.

The Indian court then acknowledged the resemblance of the Golden Passion's packaging and eventually found that the sale of such products constituted an infringement of Ferrero trade dress rights in India. The use of Ferrero Rocher's iconic shape—the High Court of Delhi continued—led consumers

---

1 See https://www.ferrero.co.uk/Ferrero-Rocher, retrieved December 22, 2023.

DOI: 10.4324/9781003433675-5

to be confused about the trade origin of the chocolates, making them erroneously believe that Ruchi was authorized to sell the chocolates in question. Because Ferrero was able to provide extensive evidence in this regard, the court was able to confirm that Ruchi was attempting to pass off their products as Ferrero's. The court took a particularly strict stance as it also held that Ruchi was weakening the Ferrero Rocher trade dress and conducting unfair competition practices to the detriment of Ferrero's rights and its business in the Indian market.

It was, thus, a total victory for Ferrero as the High Court of Delhi also awarded the company damages and ordered the manufacturer of Golden Passion chocolates to stop selling or otherwise commercially exploiting the infringing chocolates in question.

This case, once again, confirmed the importance of adopting a highly recognizable trade dress in the food world. Essential to this idea is that certain products have a look and feel that immediately sets them apart from other products. While look and feel are not unequivocally definable, they typically encompass aspects such as the shape, the color, the packaging, the imagery, and the overall feel of a product, possibly including the temporal and qualitative aspects of the gustatory experience.

Trade dress is comparable to imagery (e.g., logos) and words accompanying and characterizing a product. However, the richness and complexity of the idea of trade dress arguably make it the most important theoretical link between discourses on IP rights and debates in food aesthetics, broadly construed.

Sources

Delhi High Court, Ferrero Rocher v. Ruchi International CS (COMM) 76/2018, April 2, 2018.

4 Chocolate Bunnies and Reindeer

Lindt & Sprüngli v. OHIM

Between 2004 and 2005, Lindt & Sprüngli applied to (what is now) the European Union Intellectual Property Office (EUIPO) to register three-dimensional EU trademarks in the shapes of a chocolate rabbit and a chocolate reindeer wrapped in gold foil, as well as a bell on a red ribbon. However, the EUIPO rejected Lindt's registration application, based on a lack of distinctiveness regarding the shapes.

After the registrations were rejected by the EUIPO, Lindt appealed the decision by taking the matter to the EU General Court. EU trademark rules expressly provide that a sign can be registered as a trademark if it is represented graphically, including in words, by way of design or shape, and also by packaging, provided it is capable of distinguishing one undertaking's products or services from those of another. Furthermore, a mark that lacks distinctiveness cannot be registered, with the exception of a mark that has gained distinctiveness through use. In this specific case, the EU General Court had to rule on whether the marks and shapes could be used to set aside Lindt products as distinct and coming from Lindt undertakings. To determine whether the shape indicated the commercial origin of the relevant products, the court examined Lindt products for which the trademark applications had been filed and considered the average consumer's perception.

When the court examined the shapes, it found that the overall perception of Lindt products was not correlated solely with Lindt because of their particular characteristics. The court reasoned that rabbits, reindeer, bells on red ribbons, and the colors gold and red were traditional seasonal symbols used in confectionery during Christmas and Easter (due to religious connotations) and, thus, were not distinctive in a substantial part of the EU.

Lindt, on the other hand, argued that it was the only chocolatier selling such shapes of chocolate and that these shapes had already been registered as trademarks in 15 EU member states and therefore should be registrable by the EUIPO as well. However, the judges pointed out that the average customer is unlikely to make assumptions about the product's origin based on its packaging or shape if it lacks a distinctive brand name or graphic feature. As a result, establishing the distinctiveness of Lindt product shapes and other features

DOI: 10.4324/9781003433675-6

was impossible because they resembled traditional shapes such as rabbits and reindeer.

The fact that no other chocolate manufacturer sold a chocolate product shaped like a reindeer wrapped in gold foil with a red ribbon and a bell did not affect the court's decision. Since the use of foil in the confectionery industry is common and widespread, the EU General Court concluded, Lindt had not shown that a distinctive character had been acquired through use in the EU.

The decision itself was found to prevent the risk of monopolization of the shapes in question and thus provided realistic guidelines for any potential three-dimensional shape registration by confectionery manufacturers. It was an important decision for Lindt since any further infringement proceedings for violation of the mark brought by Lindt against its competitors were likely to fail.

The decision of the EU General Court implicitly suggests that to confer an iconic status to a product it is not enough to give it a generic form or to wrap it in generic materials. Trademark protection of the shapes of goods can be invoked only when consumer ability to choose products is driven by the appearance and characterizing features of the goods themselves.

Sources

General Court EU, Chocoladefabriken Lindt & Sprüngli v. OHIM, December 17, 2010, T-336/08.

5   Chocolate Squares

Ritter Sport v. Milka

In 1996 and 2001, the German confectioner Ritter Sport registered two three-dimensional trademarks in Germany protecting the square shape of "Ritter Sport" and "Ritter Sport Mini" chocolate bars. The registration was granted because the shape was considered distinctive and thus allows consumers to distinguish this product from those of competitors. The shape was chosen in 1932 by the company's co-founder, Clara Ritter. She reportedly had said: "let's make a chocolate bar that fits in everyone's jacket pocket without breaking and weighs the same as a normal long bar."

In 2010, Milka—Ritter's competitor (owned by the US confectionary company Mondelez, formerly Kraft Foods)—began selling square chocolate bars whose shape was similar to those of Ritter Sport. Milka also challenged the company's monopoly over the shape and began legal proceedings requesting the revocation of the trademarks in question. The main argument put forward by Milka was that Ritter Sport's square shape gave substantial value to its products. Indeed, German and European Union trademark laws prohibit the registration of shapes which confer value to a product, meaning that shapes of goods which have an exclusively aesthetic or ornamental value cannot be registered as trademarks.

After a ten-year battle, in 2020, the German Federal Court eventually sided with Ritter Sport, confirming that the shape—which is part of Ritter's brand history—does have characterizing features capable of allowing consumers to associate the products with Ritter Sport itself, which is the most important requirement for attracting trademark protection.

The court also held that the square shape in question does not confer value to the products and that therefore the company's trademark registrations are valid. Specifically, the German court noted that the square shape could not be considered as having specific artistic or design value. It reached this conclusion even though Ritter had implemented a marketing strategy focusing on the well-known advertising slogan "Square. Practical. Good." which instead seems to suggest that the square shape does give value to the chocolate bars. But the court insisted that the slogan did not have relevance for the value of the chocolate, although it accepted that it may have helped the shape to be

DOI: 10.4324/9781003433675-7

perceived as indicators of trade origin by consumers and thus associated with certain quality expectations.

The German court also mentioned other factors it had taken into account when concluding that the shape of Ritter Sport bars does not give the product substantial value, including the category of products, the differences between the square and other shapes, which are regularly used in the relevant markets, and the different prices of similar goods.

This is probably the most classic intellectual property dispute regarding the shape of a food product and it is an ideal starting point for conversations at the crossroad between food aesthetics, food design, and food marketing. To what extent does the shape of a product confer value to it? The German court insisted that the shape of the chocolate bar—no matter how iconic and recognizable by consumers, and no matter how widely invoked by Ritter Sport in its marketing of the product—does not confer value to the product per se. How far can such a position be extended to cover other food products? Does the shape of certain breads, for instance, confer value to them by making them easier to distribute, store, share, or consume? Also of note is the existence of products—e.g., some beverages—whose packaging is shaped so as to enhance the olfactory evaluation during consumption and, thus, heighten the overall gustatory experience.

Sources

German Federal Court of Justice, Decisions of July 23, 2020—Quadratische Tafelschokoladenverpackung II, ECLI:DE:BGH:2020:230720BIZB42.19.0.

Germany's Ritter Sport wins square chocolate battle against Milka. (2020, July 23). *BBC*. https://www.bbc.com/news/world-europe-53510219

Goh, B. (2020). German federal court of justice rejects cancellation of Ritter Sport's square shape mark for chocolate bars. *Journal of Intellectual Property Law & Practice*, *15*(12), 944–946. https://doi.org/10.1093/jiplp/jpaa165

6 Package Design and Signage

Oatly v. Glebe Farm

Oatly is a Swedish company and leader in the market of oat-based drinks as well as a key player in the broader dairy substitute market. Oatly's products have been on the market since the 1990s and have been sold under the Oatly label since around 2001. The brand experienced growth beginning in 2014, when it underwent a relaunch and market repositioning under new leadership.

Glebe Farm, on the other hand, is a Swedish company that was established in 2008. Since 2019, it has marketed a variety of gluten-free products under the Glebe Farm brand with descriptors such as "oat drink." Their marketed products include bread, breakfast cereals, and flour, as well as oat drinks. Glebe Farm decided to rebrand later in 2019, with their new oat-drink packaging hitting the shelves in January 2020 under the brand name "Pureoaty." According to Oatly, Glebe Farm's blue packaging and teacup image were changed to be more similar to its own.

In June 2020, Oatly filed a case before the High Court of London against Glebe Farm, seeking an injunction to stop Glebe Farm from allegedly infringing Oatly's registered trademarks and passing off (passing off occurs when a business passes off their goods or services as those offered by a competitor). Oatly claimed that Glebe Farm used signs, specifically "Pureoaty," and the design of its packaging similar to Oatly's registered trademarks, raising the assumption that the similarities were deliberate and that Glebe Farm's intention was to bring Oatly's products and reputation to mind, thereby benefiting Glebe Farm. Oatly also requested that all infringing products be recalled and permanently removed from stores, as well as that all infringing signs used by Glebe Farm be erased or obliterated.

In their defense, Glebe Farm stated that none of the changes to its packaging were intended to be reminiscent of Oatly products, and that it sought to establish its own identity by emphasizing Britishness and the family farm aspect. Glebe Farm argued that the combination of the terms "pure" and "oaty" helps define the product's qualities and is a play on the word "purity," and that the cartons marketed by the two companies in question appear different, causing no consumer confusion. Glebe Farm also argued that because

DOI: 10.4324/9781003433675-8

of differences in naming, graphical components, and presentation, marks and signs could be easily distinguished.

In June 2021, the judge ruled in favor of Glebe Farm. The court acknowledged Oatly's strong brand and distinctiveness, but determined that the few existing similarities between the signs and the packaging were insufficient to rule in Oatly's favor as there is no risk of confusion on the part of consumers. Specifically, the judge observed that:

> Oatly's marks have a strong reputation and […] there is an identity of the parties' goods. I also accept that use of the PUREOATY sign is likely to bring the Oatly marks to the minds of many average consumers (if only because the product is an oat drink and an average consumer would be well aware of Oatly's importance in that market). On the other hand, there is a relatively low or, at best, very modest level of similarity between the sign and the marks and that similarity is due to the presence in both the sign and the mark of the letters "OAT" that are descriptive of the relevant products.

The judge also expanded on the alleged conceptual similarity between the two terms in question. He argued:

> [i]t seems to me that […] the average consumer would see the degree of conceptual similarity as being low to moderate at best and as deriving from the presence in both the sign and the marks of the descriptive word "OAT."

Sources

High Court of Justice Business and Property Courts of England and Wales, August 5, 2021, EWHC 2189 (IPEC), Claim No. IP-2020-000059, Oatly AB v. Glebe Farm Foods.

Part II
Genericity and Descriptiveness

7 Feta Cheese

Feta is a Greek cheese produced from sheep's and goat's milk. It is well known for its tangy, sharp flavor and creamy texture. It has been made in Greece for centuries, with some sources even dating back its initial production to 6,000 years ago. Greece is also the largest feta cheese consumer, accounting for the highest annual consumption in the European Union (EU). In the 1930s, Greece established specific rules of production for the cheese to make sure that also in the future it would be made according to traditional techniques. Then, in 1994, a Greek law confirmed that the milk used for producing feta must exclusively come from goats and sheep in Central and West Macedonia, Epirus, Thrace, Central Greece, Thessaly, the Peloponnese, and the island of Lesbos based on the rather common opinion, when it comes to geographical indications, that a mix of "local" climatic conditions and production techniques gives the product a specific composition and some specific organoleptic properties.

In 1994, Greece also began a lengthy process to obtain geographical indication (GI) protection in the EU for its feta cheese and did obtain the Protected Designation of Origin (PDO) in 1996. It should also be noted that the term "feta" is not a geographical name. It is not the name of a Greek city, region, or island. The expression comes from the Italian word *fetta*, which means *slice*. Yet, "feta" is protected as if it were a geographical term as it has been traditionally considered part of Greek gastronomic culture. As also noted by the Court of Justice of the European Union (CJEU) Advocate General in the EU case Budejovický Budvar:

> [g]eographical indications and even designations of origin do not always consist of geographical names. They are called "direct" when they do and "indirect" when they do not, provided the indication or designation at least informs consumers that the foodstuff to which it relates comes from a specific place, region, or country [...] the word "cava" [...] calls to mind the Spanish [...] birthplace of a sparkling wine [...] and that "feta" identifies a Greek cheese.

The feta PDO registration was challenged by other EU states, in particular France, Germany, and Denmark, on grounds of the term being the generic name

DOI: 10.4324/9781003433675-10

for milk cheese that is stored in brine (like other generic names for cheese such as Cheddar). Those three European countries had a clear vested interest, as some of their cheesemakers used to produce large amounts of feta-labeled products for export purposes. It should also be noted that such feta-labeled products contained cow's milk (not solely sheep's and goat's milk) as well as coloring agents that modified the yellow tint deriving from such milk, and made it whiter.

The challenge was successful and the PDO was annulled in 1999. But, after additional legal proceedings, in 2005 the CJEU finally confirmed that "feta" cannot be considered a generic term for the product, and that it is a valid Greek PDO instead.

Why did the CJEU finally rule that the expression "feta" cannot be considered generic? First, the court noted that Greek national laws regulating the use of the name were relevant, as they embodied in the local legislation the traditional use of the term "feta." On the other hand, the fact that Denmark and Germany both had legislation protecting the generic use of "feta" in relation to that kind of cheese was deemed irrelevant.

More importantly, the court relied on surveys of consumers across the EU, which showed that the majority of them associated the name "feta" with the Greek cheese. This was considered conclusive. The CJEU also pointed out that in those European countries where non-Greek feta-labeled cheese was produced, the product was regularly sold with packaging showing Greek traditional imagery, which confirms that consumers in those countries consider feta as a cheese associated with Greece, even though, it had been manufactured in another country. Specifically, the CJEU noted that:

> [t]he information provided to the Court indicates that the majority of consumers in Greece consider that the name "feta" carries a geographical and not a generic connotation. In Denmark, by contrast, the majority of consumers believe that the name is generic. The Court does not have any conclusive evidence regarding the other Member States. The evidence adduced to the Court also shows that, in Member States other than Greece, feta is commonly marketed with labels referring to Greek cultural traditions and civilisation. It is legitimate to infer therefrom that consumers in those Member States perceive feta as a cheese associated with the Hellenic Republic, even if in reality it has been produced in another Member State. Those various factors relating to the consumption of feta in the Member States tend to indicate that the name "feta" is not generic in nature.

Sources

Court of Justice EU, Federal Republic of Germany (C-465/02) and Kingdom of Denmark (C-466/02) v. Commission of the European Communities, October 25, 2005.

8 Parmesan Cheese

Parmigiano Reggiano is an Italian cheese that is well known worldwide. Written records documenting the fame of "Parma's cheese" date back to the 1200s and even Giovanni Boccaccio, in his *Decameron* (circa 1350), uses the image of a mountain of grated "parmigiano" (day VIII, novel III). The production techniques for Parmigiano cheese seem to have been perfected by Benedictine monks working with cattle breeding and cheese manufacturing in the Emilia-Romagna area during the Middle Ages. One of the most distinctive techniques consisted in double-heating the milk to come up with a pasty consistency that would be hardened into compact cheese drums—a technique which is still used in contemporary Parmigiano Reggiano cheese-making.

The actual name "Parmigiano Reggiano" was coined in 1934 by the Italian inter-provincial consortium—i.e., Consorzio del Formaggio Parmigiano Reggiano—which manages and supervises the production of the cheese. The cheese was granted protected status in 1954, was then registered as an Appellation of Origin under the Lisbon Agreement in 1969, and achieved European Union (EU) Protected Designation of Origin (PDO) status in 1996. Throughout the decades, the consortium has had to police the market especially in Europe and took legal action against cheese producers from other countries using terms identical with or similar to the PDO Parmigiano Reggiano.

One of these cases originated in Germany. In 2003, the European Commission requested the German authorities to make sure that cheeses named "Parmesan" (which were not produced in the designated Italian area and thus not in accordance with the PDO specification) not be sold in Germany. The German government did not comply. While it admitted that the name has its roots around the Italian town of Parma, Germany believed that "Parmesan" had become a generic name describing that specific type of hard cheese. The case was eventually referred to the Court of Justice of the European Union (CJEU) which, in February 2008, rejected Germany's point that the term had become generic. This means that the unauthorized use of the name "Parmesan" for cheeses produced outside the designated area in Italy constitutes a PDO infringement and that the PDO owner, the Consorzio del

DOI: 10.4324/9781003433675-11

Formaggio Parmigiano Reggiano, can prevent the use of the translated term "Parmesan" in the EU in relation to any cheese produced outside the relevant geographical area in Italy. The CJEU also pointed out that cheeses distributed on the German market under the name Parmesan often include references to Italian cultural landscapes and traditions on their packaging, which may make consumers believe that the cheese is somehow associated with Italy, even if in fact it is manufactured somewhere else.

The CJEU also highlighted the factors that should be considered when determining if a term has become generic: namely, the areas where the product is manufactured; its consumption and how the name is perceived by consumers; the existence of laws regulating that product and its trade; and the way the term has been used in the EU. And it noted that Germany had not satisfied these factors—it just highlighted some quotations from dictionaries and specialist literature suggesting an alleged generic use of the name Parmesan.

The Italians were obviously glad about the overall outcome of this case. In fact, Italy, supported by the EU, has been constantly trying to attain some form of protection for the terms "Parmigiano Reggiano," "Parmigiano," or "Parmesan," especially via free-trade and economic partnership agreements with other countries, with different degrees of success. In particular, Italy is trying to halt the proliferation of "Parmesan" as a generic term in non-EU countries—it was successful in the EU as we have seen, but outside the EU this is more difficult. Indeed, the scenario outside Europe is different. In several countries, especially in the so-called New World (including the United States, Canada, Australia, and some Latin American countries), the term "Parmesan" has a more generic meaning, linked not only to the cheese produced in Italy; examples abound, including the Argentinian Reggianito and the Wisconsin parmesan.

Sources

Court of Justice EU, Commission of the European Communities v. Federal Republic of Germany, February 26, 2008, C-132/05.

De Roest, K., & Menghi, A. (2000). Reconsidering "traditional" food: The case of Parmigiano Reggiano cheese. *Sociologia Ruralis, 40*(4), 439–451.

Valisena, D., & Canovi, A. (2021). A tale of two plains: Migrating landscapes between Italy and Argentina 1870–1955. *Modern Italy, 26*(2), 125–140.

9   Russian Champagne[1]

In July 2021, Russian President Vladimir Putin signed an amendment to a federal law reserving the use of the Russian term for champagne—Шампанское (shampanskoye)—to sparkling wines produced in Russia. After negotiation, the amendment became effective in January 2022. The term brings to mind another similar story: "Sovietskoïé shampanskoye" is the Russian word—established under Stalin's rule in the 1920s—that describes a cheap and low-quality sparkling wine available in Russia, whose production method is different from the one used in France.

Putin's move caused a stir among French producers, as it requires them to use the generic term "sparkling wine" on the back of their bottles sold in Russia. One could indeed argue that obliging French champagne producers to add the generic term "sparkling wine" to their bottles and preventing them from using the term "shampanskoye" would violate international trademark and geographical indication (GI) rules, as enshrined in the World Trade Organization (WTO) TRIPS Agreement (Agreement on Trade-Related Aspects of Intellectual Property Rights). It may also be considered discriminatory, as only Russian producers would be able to use the Cyrillic term for champagne.

The new legislation appears to have been introduced without expert consultation. French champagne producers are protected by the above TRIPS provisions on trademarks and GIs—to which Russia is bound—and these are supposed to give French winemakers of Champagne a strong monopoly over the use of their brand.

Thus, for instance, major French producers like Moët Hennessy expressed disappointment about the new Russian provision; a general call from the industry to suspend shipments to Russia followed. The label change has cost the champagne industry hundreds of thousands of euros just to obtain the new certification as well as further laboratory testing, new barcodes, and labels for bottles. The Russian market for champagne ranks number 15 globally, but it is

---

1 This summary is based on an article authored by Enrico Bonadio and Alina Trapova entitled "How Russia is using intellectual property as a war tactic," published in *The Conversation* on March 18, 2022.

DOI: 10.4324/9781003433675-12

still important because Russians tend to buy expensive bottles. Russia imports around 50 million liters of sparkling wines and champagnes each year, 13% of which is champagne from France.

Commentators have pointed out that the new rule has a hidden protectionist rationale, favoring sparkling wine producers in the South of Russia (Krasnodar) and Crimea (which was annexed by Russia from Ukraine in 2014). The association of Russian makers of sparkling wines specified that around 250 million of their bottles are sold on the domestic market annually.

The French government entertained the possibility of starting a legal action against Russia within the WTO to defend the interests of French champagne producers. The TRIPS Agreement Article 20) explicitly prohibits individual countries from introducing special requirements—such as the obligation to translate a brand to the local language—that would "unjustifiably encumber" the use of such trademarks.

This rule was unsuccessfully invoked by opponents of an Australian measure introduced in 2012, which requires tobacco manufacturers to remove colorful, eye-catching logos from their packaging. The countries that opposed the new law were backed by major tobacco brands and claimed that imposing this requirement would be akin to a government unfairly stripping private businesses of their trademarks and could also mislead consumers and retailers. The WTO courts did not agree, saying instead that the law was a justifiable measure aimed at discouraging consumption of a harmful and deadly product.

But the new Russian law on labeling sparkling wine is different. It does not seem to have been passed with a clear public health interest in mind. What it appears to do, instead, is to satisfy the interests of Russian producers to be protected and insulated from the fierce competition with French champagne makers. As we write this book, France has not filed a complaint with the WTO yet. But if it eventually were to do so, expectations are that France would likely prevail.

Sources

The moratorium on Champagne labeling in Russia ends, but not negotiations. (2022, January 12). *Vitisphere*. Retrieved August 21, 2023, from https://www.vitisphere .com/news-95689-the-moratorium-on-champagne-labelling-in-russia-ends-but-not -negotiations.html

10 Champagne Sorbet

In 2015, the French wine trade committee Comité Interprofessionnel du Vin de Champagne (CIVC) sued the German supermarket chain Aldi in Germany for selling a frozen sorbet called Champagner Sorbet, which allegedly infringed the world-famous Champagne Protected Designation of Origin (PDO). The heart of the dispute concerned the exploitation of the reputation of Champagne by Aldi. Indeed, as mentioned earlier in this volume, European Union (EU) law gives PDOs generous protection by allowing their owners to prevent unauthorized parties from exploiting the evocative power of the protected names. The CIVC argued that the expression "Champagner Sorbet" conveyed an image of luxury and prestige, so as to be able to take advantage of the reputation of the Champagne PDO.

The German court ruled in favor of the CIVC. The court of appeals, however, overturned the verdict, stating that there was no exploitation of the evocative power of the Champagne PDO (which appeared well visible on the product's packaging). The case was then referred by the German court to the Court of Justice of the European Union (CJEU), which suggested that, because of the added 12% of champagne in the sorbet, the word "Champagner" next to the component "Sorbet" may provide essential characteristics to the product.

The CJEU also referred to the European Commission's Guidelines on the labeling of foodstuffs using protected geographical indications as ingredients. It noted, in particular, that the "essential characteristics" of the product should be taken into account, referring in this specific instance to the taste or aroma of the ingredient. These Guidelines require that the percentage of incorporation of the protected ingredient should "ideally be indicated in or in close proximity to the trade name of the relevant foodstuff or [...] in the list of ingredients." In other words, the Guidelines set forth three conditions for discerning whether a PDO can be incorporated in the name of a foodstuff containing products benefiting from that PDO: (1) "the foodstuff in question should not include any other comparable ingredient"; (2) "this ingredient should also be used in sufficient quantities to confer an essential characteristic on the foodstuff concerned"; (3) "the percentage of incorporation should be indicated in close proximity to the trade name."

DOI: 10.4324/9781003433675-13

In light of these Guidelines, the CJEU noted, the use of the word "Champagne" as part of "Champagner Sorbet" could be considered as an exploitation of the reputation of a PDO. But did such an exploitation give Aldi an undue advantage? This was the second prong of the test. While the CJEU pointed out that even if the quantity of champagne in the product were significant, that in itself would not be enough to establish an undue advantage. It would also be necessary to conduct a qualitative analysis, namely to verify whether the product incorporated a taste or aroma that is primarily attributed to Champagne as one of its essential characteristics, in which case the use of such a PDO in Champagner Sorbet—the CJEU held—could not be considered as taking undue advantage. Specifically, the CJEU noted:

> [w]here the name of the foodstuff indicates [...] that it contains an ingredient protected by a PDO, which is intended to convey the taste of the foodstuff, the taste imparted by that ingredient must constitute the essential characteristic of that foodstuff. If the taste of the foodstuff is more attributable to other ingredients it contains, the use of such a name will take unfair advantage of the reputation of the PDO concerned. Thus, in order to determine whether the champagne contained in the product at issue [...] confers on it one of its essential characteristics, the national court must ascertain, in the light of the evidence before it, whether the taste of the product is attributable primarily to the presence of champagne in the composition of the product. [...] the use of a PDO as part of the name under which is sold a foodstuff that does not correspond to the product specifications for that PDO but contains an ingredient that does correspond to those specifications, such as "Champagner Sorbet," constitutes exploitation of the reputation of a PDO [...] if that foodstuff does not have, as one of its essential characteristics, a taste attributable primarily to the presence of that ingredient in the composition of the foodstuff.

Sources

Court of Justice EU, Comité Interprofessionnel du Vin de Champagne v. Aldi Süd Dienstleistungs-GmbH & Co.OHG, December 20, 2017, C-393/17.

11 Tequila

Heineken is a large beer manufacturer and producer based in the Netherlands. Its *Desperados beer*, which has been on the market since 1996, is a tequila-flavored product available in the Netherlands, France, the United Kingdom, Spain, Germany, and several other countries. Desperados beer contains a specific amount of Tequila imported from a CRT-regulated manufacturer and is labeled in line with all necessary rules and regulations. The CRT (Consejo Regulador del Tequila/Tequila Regulatory Council) is Mexico's association overseeing Tequila compliance and regulations. Tequila, in fact, has been registered as a geographical indication (GI) in Mexico since 1978 under the Lisbon Agreement and in the European Union (EU) as a Protected Designation of Origin (PDO) since 2019.

In 2019, the CRT filed a lawsuit against Heineken in the Netherlands, complaining about its Desperados beer featuring the term "Tequila" on the front of its label. Specifically, the CRT argued that Heineken should cease and desist labeling and selling its beer as "Tequila," even though Heineken did advertise and describe its beer as "flavored with Tequila." The CRT argued that Tequila could not be an essential part of Desperados beer (unless 25%–51% of the product were Tequila) and thus did not comply with the Mexican production regulations applicable to Tequila products under the EU law. The CRT also argued that Heineken profited from Tequila's reputation as a registered GI and engaged in misleading advertising and unfair trading practices.

Heineken countered that the CRT lacked legal interest and therefore could not file a claim in Dutch courts while relying on Mexican regulations. On the issue related to misleading advertising practices, Heineken claimed that the CRT was neither Heineken's competitor nor customer and thus could not have a valid claim against them.

The court dismissed the CRT's claims, ruling that the beer did contain Tequila, sourced from CRT-approved Tequila makers, and therefore did not mislead customers. The court also confirmed that though the word "Tequila" appeared prominently on the front of Desperados beer packaging, a reasonable consumer would understand that Tequila is solely used for flavor and that the percentage of Tequila used in beer production is low.

DOI: 10.4324/9781003433675-14

The labeling on the bottle also complied with the labeling rules—the court said—because it clearly indicated the beer being flavored with Tequila. The court, however, did not clarify whether Desperados beer contained enough Tequila for the beer to have the essential characteristics of Tequila, leaving it unclear whether Heineken could continue to label the front of Desperados with "Tequila."

Despite the fact that the court left the crucial point unanswered, Heineken did win the lawsuit. It should also be noted that, after the dispute, Heineken rebranded its beer on the front of the bottle from "Tequila" to "Flavored with Tequila."

In July 2020, the European Commission initiated an examination procedure following a complaint on obstacles to trade within the meaning of EU Regulation 2015/1843 applied by Mexico consisting of a measure affecting the import of Tequila. In May 2021, the Commission finalized the review proceedings and concluded that:

> while the measure raises concerns on Mexico's compliance with WTO rules, specifically the prohibition of export restrictions, it is subject to a number of pending administrative proceedings that may lead to the measure's revocation or modification. Therefore, the Commission will continue to monitor the outcome of the various proceedings and, depending on their outcome, it may re-evaluate the actions to take.

In July 2021, the CRT and Heineken finally reached an amicable agreement over the use of the word "Tequila" in Desperados beer. Though the terms of the agreement are confidential, it has been reported that it benefits both parties, ensuring that the term "tequila" remains protected in the EU.

Sources

Arguijo Rodríguez, V. (2021, July 15). CRT and Heineken amicably end their dispute over the use of the word "Tequila" in desperados beer. *The IPKat*. https://ipkitten. blogspot.com/2021/07/crt-and-heineken-amicably-end-their.html

Commission Implementing Decision (EU) 2022/161, of February 3, 2022.

12 Mānuka Honey

This dispute concerns the sales of jars of mānuka honey that are labeled "100% New Zealand Mānuka Honey" by the American chain of grocery stores Trader Joe's. Mānuka honey has been used as a traditional remedy by the indigenous Māori people for centuries. However, bees do not only visit just one species of flower, and part of the pollen in that honey originates from plants other than the mānuka flower.

In a class action filed in federal court in California in 2018, the plaintiffs Lynn Moore, Shanque King, and Jeffrey Akwei claimed that Trader Joe's deceptively marketed its honey as "Mānuka Honey," despite the fact that samples tested indicated that the honey only contained between 57.3% and 62.6% mānuka pollen. To succeed in a false advertising claim (under California, New York, and North Carolina laws), the plaintiffs had to show that the honey's label was likely to be misleading and deceptive to a large part of the general consumer population or targeted consumers.

The court recognized that the statement "100% New Zealand Mānuka Honey" had some ambiguity. The court had to assess if additional easily available information to consumers would address the issue in question: "deceptive advertising claims should take into account all the information available to consumers and the context in which that information is provided and used."

In its ruling, the court noted that a reasonable honey consumer is expected to understand that honey cannot be made from a single source. It further stated that if a consumer is aware of the various percentages of mānuka indifferent mānuka honeys, it cannot reasonably expect a jar of ā100%" mānuka hoāey to cost only $13.99. The court also pointed out that such consumers would not expect Trader Joe's labels to advertise something that was impossible to source.

The court therefore dismissed the case, ruling that the label was not deceptive and in accordance with the guidelines of the US Food and Drug Administration. Nevertheless, the plaintiffs appealed the ruling, but the appeal was dismissed on the same grounds: a reasonable consumer—the court further held—could not conclude that "100% New Zealand Mānuka Honey"

DOI: 10.4324/9781003433675-15

reflects a claim that the product exclusively contains honey produced from mānuka. Specifically, the court noted:

> a reasonable consumer could not be left with the conclusion that "100% New Zealand Mānuka Honey" represents a claim that the product consists solely of honey derived from mānuka. Rather, a reasonable consumer would be left only with the conclusion that "100% New Zealand Mānuka Honey" means that it is 100% honey whose chief floral source is the mānuka plant, which is an accurate statement [...] Moreover, Trader Joe's cannot reasonably be said to have claimed in its ingredient statement that the percentage of honey derived from mānuka flower nectar is 100%. Reasonable consumers would understand that Trader Joe's listing Mānuka honey as the sole ingredient merely represents the accurate statement that mānuka honey is the only ingredient, i.e., that there are no additives or other honeys present in the product, not that it is exclusively derived from mānuka. Thus [...] [the law] does not preclude Trader Joe's from listing mānuka honey as the sole ingredient.

What is notable about this judgment is the court's conclusion that a reasonable consumer should be skeptical of advertising and, if necessary, conduct additional research to ensure the label is properly understood.

Sources

Moore v. Trader Joe's Co., No. 19-16618, July 15, 2021, (9th Cir. 2021).

Part III

Language Traps

13 Alaska Water

The German company RhönSprudel challenged a trademark consisting of the term "Alaska" and the image of a polar bear on an ice floe. The trademark was registered by the company Schwarzbräu in 1998 in relation to non-alcoholic beverages including fruit juices. RhönSprudel's argument was that the mark misled the average consumer because it had a different geographical origin from what the overall mark—both the word and figurative elements—seemed to suggest. Indeed, the beverages in question did not originate in Alaska.

The European Union (EU) General Court confirmed the earlier decision of the EU Intellectual Property Office (EUIPO) and that the trademark in question could be kept in the trademark register. The cancellation action brought by RhönSprudel was thus rejected. Specifically, the court found that consumers could not mistake the mark "Alaska" with the targeted product, citing these reasons:

> [f]irst, there is nothing to indicate that that public associated Alaska with the production of mineral and aerated waters or that of other non-alcoholic beverages. [...] On the other hand, it must be considered that the relevant public also did not associate Alaska with the production of fruit drinks, fruit juices, syrups and other preparations for making drinks, these being based on fruits and aromatic plants, since they are not produced there, in particular because of the climatic conditions. [...] It should also be noted that there is nothing to indicate that the relevant public was accustomed or would acquire the habit of associating geographical designations of distant regions of America, Africa or Asia with indications of the geographical origin of mineral water, sparkling water and even other non-alcoholic drinks.

Although a polar bear on an ice floe is a reference to the cold American state of Alaska, the court nonetheless held that elements calling to mind coldness and freshness do not necessarily cause the average consumer to associate products thus adorned as being from Alaska. The target consumers would therefore not be led to believe that the beverages at issue came from Alaska. In other words,

DOI: 10.4324/9781003433675-17

the public would think the sign to be merely evocative (recalling freshness) rather than the erroneous indication of a geographical provenance.

The EU General Court, however, also noted:

> [f]urthermore, as regards fruit-based drinks, fruit juices, syrups and other preparations for making drinks, it should be noted that [...] it is not unlikely that, in the future, a link between Alaska and those goods could be established in the eyes of the relevant public, allowing it to consider that those goods originated in Alaska.

The decision, in other words, rests on contextual elements, i.e., on the semantic powers the term "Alaska" has for consumers of products so labeled. To date, "Alaska" seems to generically evoke a place and a climate, rather than describe specific qualities of a product conferred by its geographical location. Yet, things may change and the semantics of "Alaska" may acquire a new status.

As tracking of commercial distribution of goods as well as of consumer behavior becomes more precise, linguistic analyses of how consumers respond to certain terms can become more exact as well as more readily available to companies and courts.

Sources

EU General Court, Mineralbrunnen RhönSprudel Egon Schindel v. OHIM, July 8, 2009, T-226/08.

14 Maestro Swiss

Maestro Swiss is a Malaysian company that produces and sells various types of chocolates under different brand names including "Vochelle" and "Maestro Swiss." It was involved in a litigation before the courts of Malaysia against Kraft Foods and Nestle Suisse.

Kraft Foods and Nestle Suisse are members of the Swiss trade association Chocosuisse Union des fabricants suisses de chocolat. The latter is a Swiss cooperative trade association responsible for protecting the name and goodwill of its members, who are Swiss chocolate makers.

Both Kraft Food and Nestle Suisse had been supplying chocolate to Malaysia for many years. In 2012, together with the above trade association, they filed an action with the High Court of Malaysia in Kuala Lumpur, claiming that Maestro Swiss had wrongfully used the mark "Maestro Swiss" in connection with chocolates. Specifically, they argued that such use of the mark was causing consumer misrepresentation and deception as to the true origin of the chocolate products. Indeed, they stressed that the chocolates in question were manufactured in Malaysia and contended that Maestro Swiss's actions had resulted in an extended form of passing off.

The action was eventually rejected by the Malaysian court because Chocosuisse Union des fabricants suisses de chocolat had no *locus standi* to be a party since they did not create or provide chocolates in Malaysia and therefore had no commercial interest or goodwill to protect. Furthermore, the court determined that there was no deception and that "Maestro Swiss" was a unique phrase in Malaysia regardless of its reference to Switzerland. The court of appeals, however, reversed the judgment and confirmed that Chocosuisse Union des fabricants suisses de chocolat had the necessary *locus standi* under common law and the Malaysian Geographical Indications Act (GIA), 2000.

Maestro Swiss filed an appeal with Malaysia's federal court, which was followed by another appeal by Chocosuisse, Kraft Foods, and Nestle Suisse. In 2016, this court found the GIA applicable with respect to actions completed before the legislation came into force (which was on August 15, 2001), whereas the claimants were seeking to prevent Maestro Swiss from continuing to use the logo after the GIA 2000 came into effect. Furthermore, Maestro

DOI: 10.4324/9781003433675-18

Swiss was not to be counted on to use the logo in good faith since the use was found to have intended the connection to Switzerland.

This case reinforces the importance of consumer perception of a product when it comes to court decisions. In fact, the ultimate verdict was based on information supplied by the claimants Chocosuisse, Kraft Foods, and Nestle Suisse proving that the words "Maestro Swiss" deceived and confused certain members of the Malaysian public into assuming that the products were linked to Switzerland.

This case is significant in terms of the applicability of passing off in extended form for a class of goods with value and recognized goodwill. The ruling also provided much-needed clarity in Malaysia on the relevant principles and interpretation of local legislation protecting geographical names under the GIA. At the same time, the case additionally urges the need for a more thorough study of the cultural nuances, as consuming practices vary across geographical areas and sub-communities.

Sources

Maestro Swiss Chocolate Sdn. Bhd. & 3 Ors v. Chocosuisse Union des fabricants suisses de chocolate & 2 Ors & Another Appeal (FCCA No. 02(f)-97-12-2012(W).

15 Thunder Beast

The Texan social entrepreneur Stephen Norberg originally manufactured and bottled his root beer out of TasteLab, i.e., a food incubator in Washington DC. He named his company Thunder Beast, which is a Plains Indian word for bison. The Plains Indians brewed a sassafras drink that was a predecessor to root beer. Norberg developed a variety of root beer flavors as well as a cream soda. He began selling his drinks at Harris Teeter, an American supermarket chain, as well as other locations in four states, including Washington DC.

Monster Beverages Corp., an energy drink manufacturer with a market capitalization of $47.54 billion as of October 1, 2021, petitioned the US Trademark Office in early 2016 to cancel the Thunder Beast trademark, which had been registered by Norberg's company. Monster claimed ownership of the term "beast" and the slogan "Unleash the Beast," stating that Norberg's brand was too similar and could confuse consumers looking for a Monster energy drink. In response, Thunder Beast began using the phrase "Fight monsters" on its website and on the packaging of its bottles. Norberg also hired Eve Brown, a Boston attorney who had previously represented eight other businesses targeted by Monster trademark claims. In 2018, Monster dropped its petition with the US Trademark Office and began a court case in California against Thunder Beast, claiming malicious and fraudulent acts. It also argued that the use of "Fight monsters" was trademark infringement.

Norberg defended his Thunder Beast brand, claiming that Monster's accusations were unfounded because Thunder Beasts was not even in the energy drink market. Norberg's cream soda and handcrafted root beer contain no caffeine or other popular energy drink ingredients. His tenacity eventually paid off. In November 2019, Norberg's company successfully settled the case, keeping its "Thunder Beast" trademark, with Monster waiving all compensatory claims and allowing Thunder Beast to use the "Fight Monsters" brand. Before the settlement, there was an interim decision by the Californian court finding no risk of confusion on the part of consumers:

[b]alancing the marks' visual similarities and the aural and definitional similarities between defendant's BEASTUP mark and plaintiff's marks

DOI: 10.4324/9781003433675-19

incorporating the word BEAST more heavily than the marks' visual dissimilarities, the similarity factor weighs against a finding of likelihood of confusion.

In addition, the court provided a comprehensive list of elements that can be jointly regarded as decisive in determining where the risk of confusion on the part of consumers may lie:

> [w]hen viewed in the context in which they appear in the marketplace, the marks contain noticeable and distinct differences in their display of the term "BEAST," capitalization, font, color scheme, design elements, orientation and location on the can, and prominence.

The legal dispute, which lasted more than three years, cost almost $75,000 to Thunder Beast. It required depositions in Washington DC and Boston, as well as mediation sessions in Boston and Los Angeles. Thunder Beast was delighted to have successfully defended its trademarks against Monster, which was named one of the world's top "trademark bullies" by the World Trademark Review in 2015 for utilizing its trademarks to intimidate and harass other emerging businesses.

Sources

Monster Energy Company v. Thunder Beast LLC *et al.*, case number 5:18-cv-01367 (California Central Court), November 5, 2019.

16 Prosecco v. Prošek[1]

Prosecco is probably the most famous Italian wine, a byword for sparkling good times and popping corks. But Italy is currently in a dispute over whether Croatia can sell a premium dessert wine by the name of Prošek across the European Union (EU). Prošek is made from white grapes grown mainly in the southern region of Dalmatia, using a traditional process that involves sun-drying them on straw mats before they are pressed. This wine sells at a premium because it uses many more grapes per bottle than countless other dessert wines, but the name has been banned across the EU since 2013 because of objections from the Italians. Instead, the wine trades under the name Vino Dalmato.

Croatia has been battling to have this verdict overturned ever since. To the fury of Italy, the European Commission has followed up on a recent application by Croatia for Prošek to be granted Protected Designation of Origin (PDO) status. Italian Prosecco has enjoyed this standing since 2009, as well as being protected under Italian law since 1969, and Italians believe it is unfair for the EU to consider giving equivalent protection to Prošek.

Croatia tried to begin the registration procedure to obtain PDO status for Prošek in 2013, the year it joined the EU. This was declined by the European Commission, which noted at that time that the registration could conflict with the Prosecco PDO—even though the two products are completely different. The Balkan state argues that Prošek is part of the country's heritage, dating back to before Roman times. The Croatian wine was traditionally produced domestically—made according to family recipes. It is common that when children are born in Croatia, the parents keep that year's Prošek to be consumed on their offspring's wedding day. What Prošek does not have, however, is the international commercial brand of Prosecco, whose sales have been rising strongly even in spite of the recent pandemic. There was a 17% increase in exports of Prosecco in the first four months of 2021, with total production of more than 600 million bottles a year.

1 This summary is based on an article authored by Enrico Bonadio and Magali Contardi entitled "Prosecco or Prošek? The EU battle between Italy and Croatia over wine branding," published in *The Conversation* on September 27, 2021.

DOI: 10.4324/9781003433675-20

Prosecco, too, is part of a very long tradition. Prosecco is the name of a village close to the town of Trieste, situated in the northeastern part of the Italian Peninsula from which the famous Italian sparkling wine "Prosecco" takes its name. During ancient Roman times, the village of Prosecco was home to a castle known as "castellum Pucinum," and in the old days, the wine was also known as *pucinum*, taking the name of a nearby castle. The Roman natural philosopher Gaius Plinius Secundus wrote that the Roman empress Augusta attributed her longevity to drinking this wine. The region surrounding Conegliano, in the adjacent Veneto region, has also long served as a significant area for the production of this wine, a tradition that continues to this day.

Since the name "Prosecco" has been protected by an EU PDO since 2009 and under Italian law dating back to 1969, if Italy can persuade the European Commission that the average EU consumer may believe that Prosěk is sold by Italian producers of prosecco (and thus be confused), or that Prosěk is effectively the translated Croatian term for prosecco, it would be successful in blocking Croatia's application. But the European Commission has justified the Croatian application on the grounds that two similar-sounding names can both be protected in principle, so long as confusion can be avoided. This is also the argument brought forth by Croatia during the current proceedings, in addition to highlighting the centuries-old history of its wine.

At the time of writing, the dispute is still pending. On their part, of course, the Italians will keep fighting the Croatian application even though it is hard to imagine that allowing Prosěk to be registered in the EU would do any damage to prosecco sales. The two products have different markets. Yet, Italy understandably fears that if the European Commission grants equivalent PDO status to Prošek, it could set a dangerous precedent that could leave room for a proliferation of foreign—"Italian-sounding"—products in the future.

Sources

Bonadio, E., & Contard, M. (2021, September 27). Prosecco or prošek? The EU battle between Italy and Croatia over wine branding. *The Conversation.* https://theconversation.com/prosecco-or-prosek-the-eu-battle-between-italy-and-croatia-over-wine-branding-168759

Bonadio, E., & Contardi, M. (2022). The GI prosecco battle between Italy and Australia: Some lessons from the history and geography of the most famous Italian wine. *Journal of World Trade & Investment, 23*(2), 260–292.

17 Ethiopian Coffee

Ethiopia's economy relies heavily on the coffee trade. Coffee also constitutes a cultural heritage asset for this African country, considered by many to be the birthplace of the coffee plant. In 2004, the Ethiopian government started an initiative called the Ethiopian Coffee Trademarking and Licensing Initiative with the intent of fixing the divide between what coffee farmers obtain for producing beans and what distributors pay when selling the final product in retail environments in other countries. This licensing scheme is managed by a consortium called Fine Coffee Stakeholder Committee, which includes private Ethiopian exporters and the Ethiopian Intellectual Property Office (EIPO). It is believed that this initiative has contributed to distinguishing Ethiopian coffee from coffees from other areas of the world. This has driven up the demand for coffee from Ethiopia in the global market, thus allowing local producers to set the price of the product themselves, increasing their revenue and raising their own standards of living.

In 2004, the Ethiopian government also requested the US coffee giant Starbucks withdraw its application to register the name "Shirkina Dun-Dried Sidamo" as a US trademark. Moreover, it launched an initiative to protect and differentiate their Harrar, Sidamo, and Yirgacheffe coffees relying on intellectual property (IP) rights, especially trademarks, to generate higher returns from coffee resellers and retailers.

It should be noted that Ethiopia has not yet implemented a system of geographical indication (GI) protection for these designations, mainly due to the cost and impracticality of such a regime. For example, under that scheme Sidamo coffee would have had to be processed in a specific region of the country and using specific methods, giving it a distinct flavor. The government would also have had to track coffee producers and distributors to ensure that the coffee truly came from those particular regions. Since the majority of the coffee is carried for several miles on foot, delivery and distribution would have been difficult as well.

As an alternative, the Ethiopian government opted for a trademark registration strategy, also abroad. The aim was to try to exploit brands via licensing so as to allow farmers to raise their prices and eventually export more

DOI: 10.4324/9781003433675-21

coffee, which would eventually increase their revenue. Thus, in 2005, the Ethiopian government filed trademark applications for the coffee-related names "Harrar," "Sidamo," and "Yirgacheffe" at the EIPO. It also filed applications in the United States, Canada, the European Union, Australia, Brazil, South Africa, China, and Saudi Arabia. While the US Trademark Office accepted the application for "Yirgacheffe," it rejected those for "Harrar" and "Sidamo." Indeed, the US National Coffee Association (allegedly lobbied by Starbucks) had opposed those applications, claiming that the names in question are generic and describe the product. The US Trademark Office refused the registration of the Harrar application in 2005 and the Sidamo application in 2006.

The EIPO successfully fought these rejections by bringing evidence to show that the names in question had instead become distinctive enough to deserve trademark protection. Both the Harrar and Sidamo trademarks were finally registered in the United States by the Ethiopian government.

Also, in 2006, the US coffee giant Starbucks started negotiations with the Ethiopian government which eventually led to a marketing, licensing, and distribution agreement in 2007. This recognized Ethiopia's ownership of the three coffee designations "Harrar," "Sidamo," and "Yirgacheffe" both in states where trademarks are registered and countries where they are not. It also provided that Starbucks is not obliged to pay royalties for exploiting these designations. This accord has been hailed as a win-win scenario, which has increased the popularity of Ethiopian coffee as well as met the expectations of a major multinational coffee company.

The post-agreement statements from the Ethiopian government and Starbucks were emblematic. The EIPO director at that time stated:

> Ethiopia is firmly committed to work in partnership with all international specialty coffee companies and distributors of its fine coffees, including Harar, Sidamo, and Yirgacheffe. We realize our approach to trademarking and licensing these coffee brands that originate in and represent the best of Ethiopia's coffee heritage is a new approach that not only meets the needs of small Ethiopian fine coffee farmers and traders but also the coffee roasting and distributing companies and their customers.

And Starbucks' chairman commented:

> Ethiopia is recognized as the historic birthplace of coffee and the source of some of the finest coffee in the world. We're extremely excited to continue to deepen our relationship with the government of Ethiopia.

This case also fits the "genericity and descriptiveness" category, as it concerns the regulation of "Harrar," "Sidamo," and "Yirgacheffe" designations as generic or specific. At the same time, the agreement attests that the negotiations surrounding the use of designations are complex international affairs. They involve stakeholders at different levels, including consumers for whom such designations may constitute a language trap—i.e., a confusing or even misleading sign. In this specific case, the generic nature and the accuracy of descriptors within different social contexts and markets posed a major problem, which was solved by establishing new trademarks rather than new geographical indications.

Sources

Seager, A. (2007, May 3). Starbucks strikes deal with Ethiopia. *The Guardian.* https://www.theguardian.com/business/2007/may/03/globalisation.money

The Coffee War: Ethiopia and the Starbucks Story. https://www.wipo.int/ipadvantage/en/details.jsp?id=2621

18 Vegan Dairies

TofuTown is a German company that produces, markets, and distributes solely plant-based goods under signs such as "Soyatoo Tofu butter," "Plant cheese," "Veggie cheese," and "Cream." The Verband Sozialer Wettbewerb is a German association specializing in fighting unfair competition, which took TofuTown before the Regional Court in Trier (Germany) and asked for an injunction prohibiting the use of those terms. It claimed that promoting products bearing those signs infringes European Union (EU) rules and legislation on designations for milk and milk products.

It should preliminarily be noted that milk and dairy products have been legally protected in the EU for decades as being distinctive in composition and source and deriving from a mammal. EU law safeguards consumers from misinformation and ensures that every citizen obtains clear knowledge and understanding regarding milk and milk products. This is also critical when it comes to the special nutritional quality that milk has by itself.

The case was then referred to the Court of Justice of the European Union (CJEU) for an answer on how the relevant EU law in question should be interpreted with regard to the use of the word "milk" and the designations of milk products. TofuTown noted that it had not violated any laws and argued that consumer perception of such designations has shifted significantly in recent years. It also claimed it would not use phrases like "butter" or "cream" on their own but only in combination with words relating to the plant source of the products in question such as "tofu butter" or "rice spray cream."

In 2017, the CJEU released its decision. It gave a rather strict interpretation of the provisions on the use of the expressions in question and concluded that terms like "milk," "cream," "butter," "cheese," and "yogurt" may solely be used for milk products that are derived from milk. It also held that these designations cannot legitimately be used on purely plant-based products unless they are specifically mentioned on a specific list of exceptions, which is not the case for soy and tofu. Simply adding a descriptive or explanatory term such as "plant cheese," "veggie cheese," "tofu butter," or "rice spray cream" does not automatically exclude consumer confusion, the CJEU decreed. Non-dairy products can only be designated by such "reserved" names under current

DOI: 10.4324/9781003433675-22

EU law when the exact meaning of the product's name is evident from traditional use (e.g., cocoa butter, cream soda, cream-filled biscuits, ice cream, butter beans) or when the designations are specifically used to identify a characteristic quality of the product (e.g., creamy).

The CJEU also clarified that purely plant-based products should not be labeled and marketed as "plant cheese" or "veggie cheese," once again confirming that dairy words like "butter" and "milk" are reserved for dairy products only. Specifically, the court noted:

> the objectives pursued by the provisions at issue consist, in particular, in improving the economic conditions for the production and marketing as well as the quality of such products. The application of such standards is therefore in the interest of producers, traders and consumers, to protect consumers and to maintain conditions for allowing competition. Those provisions, in so far as they provide that only the products which comply with the requirements they lay down can be designated by the term "milk" and the designations reserved exclusively for milk products even if those designations are expanded upon by explanations or descriptions such as those at issue in the main proceedings, contribute to the attainment of those objectives.

The European Dairy Association and all of its members welcomed the decision of the court. For many years the European dairy sector had been involved in protecting these terms and sustained the argument that milk and dairy products have a distinctive and natural class of micro- and macronutrients, which to date cannot be found in non-dairy products. Though the TofuTown decision did not ban dairy-style names for tofu and soy, it still confirmed—as we have seen—that the dairy industry has a monopoly on terms that have a quite important commercial value and affirmed that plant-based food manufacturers and producers cannot circumvent the restrictions by using a plant-based definition alongside such terms.

Sources

Court of Justice EU, Verband Sozialer Wettbewerb eV v. TofuTown.com GmbH, June 14, 2017, Case C-422/16.

19 Beyond Meat Burger

Beyond Meat Inc. is a food-processing company founded in 2009 by Ethan Brown and headquartered in the United States, which offers plant-based alternatives to beef, pork, and poultry. The company has since registered more than 100 trademarks in several countries consisting of terms such as "Beyond Meat," "Beyond Sausage," "Beyond Bacon," "Beyond Chicken," "Beyond Jerky," "Beyond Crab," "Beyond Shrimp," "Beyond Tuna," "Beyond Deli," "Beyond Bowls," "Beyond Brunch," and "Beyond Eggs," among others. These have been registered for a variety of products including those in trademark class 29 (meat substitutes) and trademark class 30 (prepared food with ingredients such as quinoa, noodles, rice, and pasta). The aim of this trademark filing strategy is to replace concepts typically associated with animals with those of plants by means of a food technology—and, obviously, to prevent competitors from using such signs in the marketplace.

According to a spokesperson for the company: "[o]ur commitment to rapid and relentless innovation means we're always working to bring the world's best plant-based meat products to market to increase accessibility to delicious, nutritious and sustainable plant-based proteins."

In January 2020, the company opposed the "Beyond Meat Burger" mark (written in katakana), which had been filed by a local individual in connection with meat products and clothing with the Japanese Trademark Office. This trademark—the US company argued—is identical with or similar to its well-known registered sign, i.e., "Beyond Meat," and could secure unfair profits for the above individual or be detrimental to the US food-processing company. The Japanese Trademark Office recognized that Beyond Meat Inc. had established a significant level of reputation as a source indication of plant-based meat replacements, also in Japan (even though the US company had yet to launch products there under that brand). It concluded that the two marks were confusingly similar and canceled the trademark "Beyond Meat Burger." Furthermore, the court found there to be reasonable grounds to believe that such a trademark application had been filed to take unfair advantage of the commercial reputation acquired by the "Beyond Meat" sign in Japan.

DOI: 10.4324/9781003433675-23

As this case shows, Beyond Meat Inc. is on top of its game in planning an effective strategy of trademark filing and enforcement aimed at monopolizing and exploiting brands which epitomize its whole mission, i.e., taking the concept of animals out of the food system.

The case is also a textbook classic for debates in food ethics. On the one hand, Beyond Meat Inc. is a pioneer company in developing products that arguably reduce animal cruelty as well as the environmental impact of consuming animals and animal products. On the other hand, the company trademark strategy also raises questions regarding perspectives and regulations circa technological advancements in food production and intellectual property rights that are granted to brands that highlight such advancements. True enough, a company should profit from its investments in innovation and its capacity to bring products to market that are sought by consumers. Yet, should technology and branding come to have such a bearing on the identity of traditional staples such as salmon, bacon, sausage, etc.?

Sources

Japanese Patent Office, Opposition case no. 2020-900023, Gazette issued: July 30, 2021.

Mikami, M. (2021, September 5). Beyond meat defeats "beyond meat burger." https://www.marks-iplaw.jp/beyond-meat-burger/

Woolfson, D. (2022, October 10). Beyond meat signals ready meals launch with trademark application. *The Grocer*. https://www.thegrocer.co.uk/new-product-development/beyond-meat-signals-ready-meals-launch-with-trademark-application/672183.article

Part IV

Procedures

20 Chemical Aging of Rum and Whiskey

Back in 2014, Lost Spirits, a Los Angeles–and Las Vegas–based distillery producing whiskey and rum, filed patent applications for protecting its spirit aging method. This method recreates the chemical signature of rum or whiskey aged in barrels for 20 years in less than a week. In 2019, Lost Spirits whiskies were selected as World Whisky of the Year in the Wizards of Whisky competition and scored the rating "Liquid Gold" in Jim Murray's Whisky Bible. The high-tech method (which breaks down oak barrel wood and uses heat and particular wavelengths of light) was granted a US patent in 2015 and an Israeli patent in 2020. Lost Spirits now owns a portfolio of patents that protects this maturation technology and has obtained patent protection in India, Japan, China, and Australia as well.

These patents were obtained as Lost Spirits has proven that its unique process of photocatalysis and photodegradation of naturally occurring wood polymers, in combination with heat-driven esterification, produces chemical changes in distilled spirits that are comparable to those that occur in oak barrels over decades.

The process is divided into three steps. During the first step, a tank is filled with white spirit and wood pieces that are heated to 140–170 °F for several days. This method forces the esterification of short-chained fatty acids, producing fruity esters. The second step, which uses light, physically breaks up big polymer molecules in the oak, eliminating the chemicals and releasing more flavorful molecules, as well as ethyl acetate. The tank is heated further in the third and final step, where the complex solution goes through further chemical reactions. The residual acids then convert to esters, resulting in rich, honeylike notes normally found in long-term barrel maturation.

The patented technology allows spirits to be produced in less than a week, but the spirit is not old per se—it only tastes like an old one. In other words, the spirit only has the characteristics associated with an old distilled spirit.

As described in the specifications of the US patent protecting this method (US Patent No. 9,637,713 B2):

DOI: 10.4324/9781003433675-25

[t]he invention pertains to processes for producing a distilled spirit having characteristics associated with a mature distilled spirit. The distilled spirit produced in accordance with the process has many of the characteristics associated with a matured distilled spirit produced in accordance with industry standards, but is advantageously produced in a shortened timeframe while eliminating the evaporation problem and greatly reducing the "off flavors" associated with excess ethyl acetate. By contacting an unmatured distilled spirit with wood at increased temperatures and contacting the spirit with actinic light, the maturation process can be shortened without reducing the quality of the spirit. In particular, it has surprisingly been found that the processes described herein produce a spirit having similar chemical markers as a 32 year-old spirit in a significantly reduced period of time.

Interestingly, the specifications also detail the problem the invention aims to solve:

[c]onsumers of distilled spirits are often educated and discerning. Many will refuse to consume or pay a premium for non-authentic tasting products. What is needed is a means by which the quality and complexities associated with traditionally aged spirits can be achieved in a significantly reduced timeframe, preferably with a reduction in the evaporation of finished goods and a reduction of the build-up of ethyl acetate.

Patenting techniques of producing alcohol are not uncommon, but the technology developed by this Californian distillery seems rather revolutionary. It is certainly a positive thing that patents are granted when breakthrough inventions are made. This is exactly what the patent system is supposed to do, i.e., encourage and reward truly innovative activities.

Sources

Method for Rapid Maturation of Distilled Spirits Using Light and Heat Processes, US Patent N0,9,637,713 B2, Inventor Bryan Alexander Davis, Current Assignee LOST SPIRITS DISTILLERY LLC. https://patents.google.com/patent/US9637713B2/en

21 Packaged Parma Ham

Parma ham is one of the most famous and finest hams in the world. Traditionally produced in and around the Italian city of Parma, it involves a long process of manufacturing. The ham is derived from the hind legs of the pig. The flesh loses a large quantity of moisture during the curing process with sea salt, i.e., typically around a quarter of its weight, just enough to preserve the gammon without making it taste overly salty. The law requires that the aging period for the preparation of the legs be at least one year, beginning on the date of the initial salting, while some may be cured for up to three years: A strong, concentrated flavor is the consequence.

The expression "Prosciutto di Parma" obtained European Union (EU) Protected Designation of Origin (PDO) status in 1996 ("prosciutto" being the Italian word for ham). But, having reached worldwide renown, Parma ham has inevitably attracted imitations, with producers and distributors from several countries other than Italy trying to use the name Parma when labeling ham. A long-running battle began in 1997 when the Italian Parma Ham Consortium sued Asda, a British supermarket chain, in the United Kingdom. The Consortium claimed that Asda was in breach of the law that states that authentic Parma ham must be sliced and packaged exclusively in the geographical area in and around the town of Parma in Italy. Asda sliced and packaged the ham in question in the United Kingdom at the meat plant near Chippenham in Wiltshire. This was driven by the supermarket's desire to keep production prices low.

The specifications for Prosciutto di Parma PDO (in English: Parma Ham) expressly require that the ham be sliced and packaged in the Parma area under the supervision of the Consortium. The latter also has the right to control and authorize the companies chosen to carry out the slicing and packaging activities. Moreover, the specification mandates strict labeling requirements. More specifically, the packaging must include: the name and brand of the manufacturers or packers and sellers; the date of production; the area of the packaging plant; and recommendations for product preservation.

The Parma Ham Consortium argued that the "Prosciutto di Parma" expression as well as the English translation Parma Ham ought to be protected (this is

DOI: 10.4324/9781003433675-26

also what the specific EU Regulations on geographical indications mandate). It also claimed that products like Parma ham are cultural artifacts reflecting a long-established cultural production. On the other hand, Asda argued that the slicing and packaging requirements were unjustified and unreasonable and constituted a barrier to the free movement of goods, which is guaranteed under EU law.

In 2003, the Court of Justice of the European Union (CJEU) ruled in favor of the Parma Ham Consortium. It held that the slicing and packaging of the ham in the designated Parma area positively affected its quality and, accordingly, the reputation of the product among consumers. Thus, the court added, while these requirements have the effect of introducing an obstacle to intra-EU trade, such a barrier is justified in order to protect the Parma Ham PDO. Specifically, the CJEU held:

> [t]he carrying out of checks helps to maintain the quality and hence also the reputation of sliced Parma ham. It might accordingly be concluded that the requirement to slice and package the ham in the region of production under the supervision of the Consorzio is justified in order to protect industrial property. [...] The requirement to slice Parma ham in the region of production can ensure, in particular having regard to the quality controls undertaken by the Consorzio, that the sliced ham consists only of Parma ham, comes from the region of production and is sliced, packaged and labeled in accordance with the rules laid down for using the PDO Prosciutto di Parma.

The CJEU also confirmed that the scope of protection given by the Prosciutto di Parma PDO includes the right to prevent companies from outside the Parma area from using the translated expression "Parma Ham." This finding does not really come as a surprise because EU law itself explicitly gives PDO holders the right to oppose the use of translations of the protected terms. The court also noted that the control over where the process of slicing and packaging takes place guarantees the quality and authenticity of the product in question.

One of the consequences of this decision was that Asda moved its Parma Ham packaging operations back to Italy from the United Kingdom.

Sources

Court of Justice EU, Consorzio del Prosciutto di Parma and Salumificio S. Rita SpA v. Asda Stores Ltd and Hygrade Foods Ltd., May 20, 2003, C-108/01.

22 The Uncrustable Sandwich

In 1897, Jerome Smucker established the J.M. Smucker Company. In 1999, the company purchased a smaller company and its patent from David Geske and Len Kretchman. This company produced crustless sandwiches. Several months following the takeover, Smucker's launched a promotional campaign for the patented sandwich, which was marketed as *Uncrustable*. It was a frozen, round, crustless sandwich filled with peanut butter and jelly. These sandwiches had gained popularity among schoolchildren due to the company's unique crimping process which sealed the bread edges. The Uncrustable's seal provided a competitive advantage over other sandwiches, including other sealed-edge sandwiches that used starch for the process.

Specifically, the invention in question (protected by a US patent) was described as follows in the patent document (abstract):

[a] sealed crustless sandwich for providing a convenient sandwich without an outer crust which can be stored for long periods of time without a central filling from leaking outwardly. The sandwich includes a lower bread portion, an upper bread portion, an upper filling and a lower filling between the lower and upper bread portions, a center filling sealed between the upper and lower fillings, and a crimped edge along an outer perimeter of the bread portions for sealing the fillings therebetween. The upper and lower fillings are preferably comprised of peanut butter and the center filling is comprised of at least jelly. The center filling is prevented from radiating outwardly into and through the bread portions from the surrounding peanut butter.

It is also interesting to highlight the problem this invention aims at solving. As mentioned in the patent document:

[t]he present invention relates generally to sandwiches and more specifically it relates to a sealed crustless sandwich for providing a convenient sandwich without an outer crust which can be stored for long periods of time without a central filling from leaking outwardly. Many individuals

DOI: 10.4324/9781003433675-27

enjoy sandwiches with meat or jelly like fillings between two conventional slices of bread. However, some individuals do not enjoy the outer crust associated with the conventional slices of bread and therefore take the time to tear away the outer crust from the desired soft inner portions of the bread. This outer crust portion is then thrown away and wasted. There is currently no method or device for baking bread without having an outer crust. Hence, there is a need for a convenient sandwich which does not have an outer crust and which is not prone to waste of the edible outer crust portions. The present invention provides a method of making a sealed crustless sandwich which can be stored for extended periods of time without an inner filling from seeping into the bread portion.

The patent, however, drew criticism, especially when in 2001 Smucker's attempted to enforce it against a small company in the Midwest named Albie's Foods which produced similar goods. It did so by issuing cease and desist letters. Albie's Foods did not comply with these letters and even filed a case against Smucker's in Michigan. Through this lawsuit, Albie's Foods sought to invalidate Smucker's patent. Then, Smucker's brought a patent lawsuit against Albie's, this time in Ohio. In this specific case, Smucker's formally accused Albie's Foods of infringing on its patent claims.

The court in Ohio compared the elements of Smucker's patent claims with Albie's Foods product. Albie's Foods argued that their goods were actually pastries and were a popular dish in northern Michigan since the 19th century. The infringement case terminated pending reexamination of the patent. Indeed, simultaneously, Albie's Foods filed a request in 2001 with the US Patent Office to reexamine Smucker's patent in light of relevant prior art (namely, lack of evidence of novelty). This was not a lawsuit, but rather a request to evaluate and reexamine patent claims in light of new information provided by Albie's Foods. The patent claims were then reviewed in light of the new reference to see if the invention was still novel, useful, and non-obvious—these are the patentability requirements under US law. The reexamination of Smucker's patent resulted in the claims of the patent itself being reduced to include just a very particular kind of crustless sandwich in response to Albie's Foods' request. The saga continued for a while, but in 2006 the US Patent Office ultimately canceled the patent mainly due to the vagueness of its claims.

Sources

Sealed Crustless Sandwich, US Patent No. 6,004,596 A. Inventors Len C. Kretchman, David Geske. Current Assignee Smucker Fruit Processing Co. https://patents.google.com/patent/US6004596A/en

23 Battered French Fries

Since 2004, batter-coated French fries are regarded as fresh vegetables by the US Department of Agriculture (USDA), together with other sliced, diced, and peeled vegetables.

According to the US Department of Agriculture, the classification only applies to trade rules and not nutrition or food safety, for the purpose of the Perishable Agricultural Commodities Act. The Act was introduced in 1930 to regulate the marketing of perishable agricultural commodities in the United States and internationally. Initially adopted during the Great Depression, the regulation provided a financial settlement mechanism for farmers, buyers, and sellers of perishable agricultural goods. It was intended to protect one party should the other party go out of business or the goods arrive at the destination spoiled or perished.

When the USDA was forced to memorialize the record according to which coating and battering of French fries should be included in that act and granted protection, there were two comments supporting this record, one of which came from a low-profile institute that did not even have a website (demonstrating that a little lobbying can go a long way).

The classification of batter-coated French fries as vegetables has enraged health advocates who regard such fries as a processed food, regardless of how the USDA justifies its approach under the Perishable Agricultural Commodities Act, but most other types of frozen fries have been on the list since 1996. The decision had immediate implications for the Texas-based Fleming Companies Inc., which before the bankruptcy had a market value of $800 million in food distribution. According to the law, fresh vegetable sellers must be paid before any other creditor, and as a result of the reclassification, Fleming's creditors filed claims under the Perishable Agricultural Commodities Act totaling $3.2 million, $1 million of which was for potato products.

Fleming then sued the USDA, claiming that the law should only be interpreted to include fresh vegetables that have not been processed, changing the food into a completely different kind or giving it a completely different character. During the court proceedings, Fleming used an expert witness and

DOI: 10.4324/9781003433675-28

shared patents that other companies had obtained in the production of batter-coated French fries, all with the goal of proving to the court that potatoes must go through many stages of processing, which eventually changes the chemical composition of the potato itself. However, Fleming lost the case.

Fleming filed an appeal in 2005, arguing that the "Batter-Coating Rule" was unlawful and that the USDA's decision-making was arbitrary and capricious, in violation of the Administrative Procedures Act. The summary judgment was denied without prejudice to renewal, which means that in the United States, French fries do not fulfill the criterion for being labeled as processed food because they are deemed fresh, affirming that the batter-coating has no effect on the US department's classification.

The case stands as a textbook paradigm to showcase the elusiveness of the idea of processed foods. While some widely used classifications—such as the NOVA food classification system—crucially rely on said idea to rank foods and encourage healthy dietary choices, the legal disputes about battered French fries flag the challenges that such classifications may run into. In fact, Braesco et al. (2022) concluded that "while the concept of ultra-processed foods has certainly entered the consumer consciousness, our results indicate that NOVA criteria do not currently allow foods to be unequivocally defined as ultra-processed."

Sources

Braesco, V., Souchon, I., Sauvant, P., Haurogné, T., Maillot, M., Féart, C., & Darmon, N. (2022). Ultra-processed foods: How functional is the NOVA system? *European Journal of Clinical Nutrition, 76*(9), 1245–1253.

Fleming Companies, Inc. v. United States Department of Agriculture, United States District Court, E.D. Texas, Sherman Division, June 4, 2004, 322 F. Supp. 2d 744 (E.D. Tex. 2004).

24 Kimchi Fermentation

The dispute began in 1996, when South Korea requested the World Health Organization and Food and Agriculture Organization Codex Alimentarius Commission to standardize the ingredients used to produce kimchi (also spelled *gimchi*, in accordance with the official Korean language romanization system adopted by South Korea). Kimchi is a popular dish of salted and fermented vegetables—most typically napa cabbage and Korean radish—though virtually any other vegetable may be used. It can be seasoned with several different flavorings, including chili powder, garlic, fish sauce, spring onions, etc.

Kimchi belongs to the generic family of pickled vegetables. Yet, it has specific ingredients and a distinctive process of production—called *kimjang* (also spelled *gimjang*)—which has been inscribed in the UNESCO Intangible Cultural Heritage repository since 2013. In Korean cuisine, kimchi is also a key element of *banchan*—a collection of small dishes that accompany diners throughout the entire meal. Kimchi has thus been a recognized national symbol of South Korea since at least the 1980s.

In the mid-1990s, a disagreement erupted between Japan and South Korea. Specifically, the latter argued that Japanese producers of kimchi substituted the traditional fermentation process with artificial flavoring and used only Chinese cabbage, without incorporating any of the ingredients commonly used in South Korea such as red pepper, garlic, or ginger. Thus, such Japanese producers did not ferment the vegetables according to established South Korean traditions and were, arguably, making a low-quality product that was not deserving of the label "kimchi" after all. South Korea thereby complained about Japan's increased production and global sales of kimchi, including imports to South Korea, alleging that no international standards were in place to inspect and assess Japanese kimchi's poor quality. The South Korean government petitioned for the need to protect consumer health and to ensure that fair trade practices be followed.

Both countries' representatives joined the Codex Alimentarius Commission meetings to discuss the issue. Over time, they agreed to establish standardized kimchi criteria in terms of its recipe and trade. South Korea preferred the conventional approach of natural fermentations, while Japan was opposed to such

DOI: 10.4324/9781003433675-29

a structural methodology. Japan also requested permission to continue export-ing kimchi to the United States due to consumer demand and because, within the US market, disputes of authenticity had never been raised, even though it meant not being able to use the word "kimuchi" (the Japanese adaptation of the Korean name kimchi) on its labels.

The South Korean government felt forced to accept a broader definition of its national dish and was therefore dissatisfied with the eventual Codex standardization of the use of citric, acetic, and lactic acids, none of which are actually used in the traditional-making process of kimchi. But as a way of compromise, in 2001, the Codex Alimentarius Commission agreed to adapt the set standard and confirmed that all countries involved in the kimchi trade would need to comply with the set rules; otherwise, kimchi could not be labeled as such.

Kimchi thus became standardized as a result of the South Korean-Japanese cooperation and compromise. The South Korean version of kimchi was inter-nationally recognized, but the extensive list of ingredients and manufacturing methods enables Japanese producers to also legally label their products as kimchi. As a result, South Korea and Japan were able to commercialize and broaden their international market for kimchi exports.

This case shows the need to devise more comprehensive and fair meth-ods for settling disputes regarding food authenticity in court. Scholarship on deliberative processes that proceed bottom up or include a mix of stakeholders (see, e.g., Feghali et al., 2022) can be of help here in future years.

Sources

Feghali, N., Piras, N., Serini, B., Borghini, A., Zara, G., Bianco, A., & Budroni, M. (2022). A deliberative model for preserving the diversity of Lebanese traditional fermented food and beverages. *Human Ecology*, *50*(3), 589–600.

Lee, J. G., Lee, Y., Kim, C. S., & Han, S. B. (2021). Codex alimentarius commission on ensuring food safety and promoting fair trade: Harmonization of standards between Korea and Codex. *Food Science and Biotechnology*, *30*(9), 1151–1170.

Surya, R., & Nugroho, D. (2023). Kimchi throughout millennia: A narrative review on the early and modern history of kimchi. *Journal of Ethnic Foods*, *10*, Article 5.

25 Smuggled Wagyu Beef

"Wagyu" is a Japanese term meaning "Japanese-style cow" and is used to identify four varieties of Japanese black cattle with unique genetic characteristics. Because of the marbling of the fat on the inside of muscle tissue, as well as massages and beer for the animals, it is recognized as one of the best quality beefs in the world. According to *Japan Times*, the Japanese government intends to double its Wagyu production from 149,000 tons in 2018 to 300,000 tons by 2035. As was to be expected, such an increase in demand resulted in a recent attempt to illegally export Wagyu genetic material from Japan to foreign countries.

In 2018, China attempted to smuggle a metal container with frozen Wagyu sperm and eggs from Osaka to Shanghai by ship. As a result, Japan's Ministry of Agriculture, Forestry, and Fisheries launched an effort to protect what it considers Japan's intellectual property (IP) and generations of selective breeding and technical know-how in Wagyu cattle eggs and sperm, fearing that Wagyu cattle would be bred in foreign countries without Japan's permission and supervision. As Japanese beef gained popularity abroad, the government grew eager to limit international production by issuing injunctions and financial penalties for using, selling, and buying illegally obtained Wagyu genetic material. It should be noted that a Chinese company called "Wagyu Bio-Tech" was founded in 2008, for breeding and producing beef in China by rearing a wagyu herd exclusively from imported embryos and semen.

A new Japanese law, which was enacted in 2020 and called "Act for Prevention of Unfair Competition Using Livestock Genetic Resources," authorizes the government to take action against Wagyu smuggling and ensure that breeders retain accurate records of fertilized eggs and sperm trading. More specifically, it allows for injunctions to be granted when genetic materials are used for breeding purposes after export and provides criteria for quantifying damages.

The legal framework put forward in this case, thus, is not strictly speaking about protecting IP rights. It is more about export controls and the need to fight unfair competition. Yet, the framework indirectly seeks to protect

DOI: 10.4324/9781003433675-30

(and ultimately is justifiable in terms of) Japan's IP in selective breeding and know-how.

The case is a sort of "old school" biotechnology dispute. Farming and agriculture crucially rely on technologies for controlling reproduction, and often possessing the right (part of the) organism to ensure proper reproduction amounts to being able to make use of the technology. A case in point is the ability of Yemeni farmers to sterilize their seeds and trade them, maintaining a market hegemony that lasted for at least two centuries until the mid-17th century. In the final part of this volume, we will look at other cases specifically focusing on biotech patents on food and legal battles over genetically modified organisms.

Another important aspect of this case is its significance to debates about the ethics of animal farming. Who should own the rights to manage, modify, and design livestock genetic resources? Should any country be entitled to such rights, or rather, should they ultimately be managed by institutions that act on behalf of the animals themselves?

Sources

Ministry of Agriculture, Forestry and Fisheries' Intellectual Property Strategy 2025. (2021, April 30). *Ministry of agriculture, forestry and fisheries of Japan.* https://www.maff.go.jp/e/policies/intel/attach/pdf/index-2.pdf

Part V

Menus, Recipes, and Creativity

26 Kim Seng v. J&A Importers

At issue in this US case from 2011 was whether the image of a "bowl-of-food" containing rice sticks, egg rolls, and grilled meat was original enough to warrant copyright. The plaintiff, Kim Seng Company, alleged that the defendant, J&A Importers Inc., had infringed the copyright on its "bowl of food sculpture" (a Vietnamese soup) by using the exact image on its packaging. In its ruling, the US court found that the bowl of food under dispute comprised unprotectable common elements that "cannot be separated from their utilitarian function, which is to be eaten" (specifically, a bowl, plus the ingredients of a traditional soup recipe). That is also why the dish lacked the originality requirement necessary for copyright protection. In other words, the court refused to consider the bowl of food an original sculpture. While this decision may make some sense, it does little to address the broader question of whether food may be used as an artistic medium, especially in an era dominated by enthusiastic cooks and foodies on social media who like to showcase their gastronomic creations.

The court also suggested that even if it had deemed the bowl sufficiently original, the latter could not be copyrighted anyway, as it would not meet the fixation requirement. In copyright law, several countries including the United States and the United Kingdom require works to be fixed on a tangible medium, which in the past has left without protection things like, for example, a make-up creation on the face of a musician, an installation of props by the pop band Oasis in and around a swimming pool, and a work of environmental art (a decorated garden in Chicago). Holding the fixation requirement unsatisfied in the Kim Seng Co. case, the court noted that the food in question was "perishable" and "once it spoils is gone forever."

A different conclusion, however, may be drawn regarding more personalized culinary creations. A case in point are so-called signature dishes in contemporary fine dining restaurants, such as "Oops! I dropped the lemon tart" by Massimo Bottura of Osteria Francescana, or the "Oysters and Pearls" and "Salmon Cornet" by Thomas Keller of the French Laundry, or the "Almond's Nougat" dessert dish, served at Quique Dacosta in Spain and described as "pure poetry." These are creations specifically designed to elicit sensorial,

DOI: 10.4324/9781003433675-32

emotional, and cognitive reactions in their consumers, which can hardly be compared to the plating presentation in Kim Seng Co. v. J&A Importers Inc. in terms of plating creativity.

Thus, even granting that the arrangement of individual elements of a dish is not copyrightable in and of itself, it is plausible to presume that, in some circumstances, such elements may embody a high degree of creativity and qualify as original (perhaps even artistic) works. This has been indirectly confirmed by the US court in the Kim Seng case. Indeed, while the court held that the copyright did not subsist in the bowl in question for lack of fixation and that the food choices were dictated by functional reasons, it also found that "the arrangement in the bowl itself was not so mechanical or routine as to require no creativity whatsoever" and that such arrangements "might demonstrate sufficient creativity to the low threshold [of originality]." After all, originality in food presentations can come in many forms. In this case, it ensued from multiple elements of a dish being selected and arranged in a way that brings about an innovative and original configuration.

The next disputes will instead focus on recipes and other procedures to make food.

Sources

Bonadio, E., & Weissenberger, N. (2022). Food presentations and recipes: Is there a space for copyright and other intellectual property rights? In A. Borghini & P. Engisch (Eds.), *A philosophy of recipes: Making, experiencing, and valuing* (pp. 199–214). Bloomsbury.

KIM SENG COMPANY, Plaintiff, v. J&A IMPORTERS, INC., et al., Defendants, August 30, 2011, Case No. CV10–742 CAS (MANx0).

Smith, C. Y. (2014). Food art: Protecting food presentation under US intellectual property law. *John Marshall Review of Intellectual Property Law, 14*, 1.

27 Lambing
v. Godiva Chocolatier

The dispute regards a claim of copyright infringement that the plaintiff and pastry chef Barbara Lambing brought against renowned chocolatier Godiva. Specifically, Lambing accused Godiva of copying both the recipe and the design of its distinctive chocolate truffle named "David's Trinidad" from one of her recipes included in her cookbook. In 1998, the US court rejected the claim noting that "[t]he identification of ingredients necessary for the preparation of food is a statement of facts" and lacks the "expressive element deserving copyright protection."

This case is similar to, but not identical with, a previous US case decided in 1996, i.e., Publications International Ltd. (this ruling was issued by the Seventh Circuit). That dispute involved a book containing 50 recipes that made use of Dannon yogurt, which was published by Meredith Corporation under the title *Discover Dannon: 50 Fabulous Recipes with Yogurt*. The contention was not about the compilation of recipes as a collective work, for which Meredith had already secured a copyright; rather, Meredith claimed that Publications International had infringed its copyright of the individual recipes by copying and using them in various publications.

Initially, the lower court found the recipes to be protected by copyright and issued an injunction order. However, the court of appeals took the opposite stance, concluding that the plaintiff's recipes could not obtain copyright because "[t]he identification of ingredients necessary for the preparation of each dish is a statement of facts" and the recipes in question did not "contain even a bare modicum of the creative expression" as is required for copyright protection. Thus, the court of appeals found that the recipes of the plaintiff and those of the defendant were substantially the same, and went on to humorously note that "it doesn't take Julia Child or Jeff Smith to figure out that the PIL [Publications International Limited] recipes will produce substantially the same final products."

Furthermore, the court of appeals defined a recipe as

a set of instructions for making something [...] a formula for cooking or preparing something to be eaten or drunk: a list of ingredients and a

DOI: 10.4324/9781003433675-33

statement of the procedure to be followed in making an item of food or drink [...] a method of procedure for doing or attaining something.

However, the court also noted that such a "mere listing of facts" stood in contrast to recipes that might "spice up the functional directives by weaving in creative narrative." This "spice," according to the deciding court, might come in the form of authors "lac[ing] their directions for producing dishes with musings about the spiritual nature of cooking or reminiscences they associate with the wafting odors of certain dishes in various stages of preparation."

Thus, in the Publications case, the court of appeals left open the question of whether and to what extent a recipe enriched via a particularly creative language may be granted copyright, simply stating that no expressive characteristics were to be found in the recipes under dispute. On the contrary, the court appointed to settling the Lambing v. Godiva case did not even consider the possibility that a recipe could include enough expressive features to make it copyrightable. What is noteworthy is that the decision regarding Publications seems more reasoned and balanced, with its approach being followed by subsequent cases on copyright and recipes. One of these is summarized in the next pages, Barbour v. Head.

Sources

Bonadio, E., & Weissenberger, N. (2022). Food presentations and recipes: Is there a space for copyright and other intellectual property rights? In A. Borghini & P. Engisch (Eds.), *A philosophy of recipes: Making, experiencing, and valuing* (pp. 199–214). Bloomsbury.

Goldman, M. (2013). Cooking and copyright: When chefs and restaurateurs should receive copyright protection for recipes and aspects of their professional repertoires. *Seton Hall Journal Sports and Entertainment Law*, *23*(1), Article 4.

Lambing v. Godiva Chocolatier, No. 97-5697, 1998 U.S. App. LEXIS 1983 (6th Cir. February 6, 1998).

28 Barbour v. Head

Judy Barbour wrote a cookbook called *Cowboy Chow* and in 1988 signed
a publishing agreement with Cookbook Resources. They subsequently sued
James Head and Penfield Press before the District Court of Southern Texas.
They argued that James Head had published—without Barbour's knowledge
or approval—an Internet magazine which included recipes virtually identi-
cal to those in Barbour's cookbook. They further contended that Penfield
Press had published the compilation cookbook *License to Cook Texas Style*,
by Dianna Stevens, which contained nearly verbatim recipes from *Cowboy
Chow*, without seeking permission from Barbour and without her knowledge.
As noted by the court:

> [f]or example, the Cowboy Chow recipe for "Cherokee Chicken" states
> in part: "Heat oil in heavy skillet. Add sugar and let it brown and bub-
> ble. (This is the secret to the unique taste!)." The virtually identical recipe
> in License to Cook Texas Style mimics this parenthetical and arguably
> expressive language, excepting the exclamation point: "Heat oil in heavy
> skillet. Add sugar and let it brown and bubble (this is the secret to the
> unique taste)." Similarly oriented anecdotal language also appears in reci-
> pes for "Crazy Horse Cranberry Sauce with Raisins," (stating "Great with
> all your meats!" in Cowboy Chow as compared to "Great with meats!"
> in License to Cook Texas Style), as well as "Pico de Gallo" (translat-
> ing "Pico de Gallo" as "Beak of the Rooster" in both books). In other
> instances, Barbour's suggestions on the presentation of food also appear in
> Defendant's book. For example, both cookbooks suggest using the "Frito"
> bag as a bowl for eating "Frito Pie," serving "Prairie Fire Dip" hot in a
> chafing dish, and filling a "glass cowboy boot mug" with "Red Beer."

Barbour and Cookbook Resources claimed that this was a case of copyright
infringement and an act of unfair competition. In particular, they argued that
the recipes were copyrightable because they were accompanied by substantial literary expression in the form of explanations, directions, and anecdotes
throughout the book as in the above-mentioned phrasing: "Heat oil in heavy

DOI: 10.4324/9781003433675-34

skillet. Add sugar and let it brown and bubble. (This is the secret to the unique taste!)."

On the other hand, James Head and Penfield Press claimed that recipes are "[m]ere listings of ingredients" and therefore not copyrightable. The court rejected James Head's arguments and found instead that recipes—when arranged in a curated collection or conveyed through substantial literary elaboration—may contain elements subject to copyright protection. Specifically, the court noted that "[o]f the twenty recipes identified [in Barbour's book] [...] as being identical or similar, the court finds that at least a few contain statements that may be sufficiently expressive to exceed the boundaries of mere fact." It added that "the recipes in Cowboy Chow are infused with light-hearted or helpful commentary, some of which also appears verbatim in License to Cook Texas Style."

On that basis, the court refused to grant summary judgment in favor of James Head. The dispute was subsequently settled. To date, however, the court's decision can be viewed as an indication of the fact that, under justified and limited circumstances, a court may be receptive to the idea of individual recipes meriting copyright.

Sources

Barbour v. Head, 178 F. Supp. 2d 758, 759, December 26, 2001, (S.D. Tex. 2001).

Bonadio, E., & Weissenberger, N. (2022). Food presentations and recipes: Is there a space for copyright and other intellectual property rights? In A. Borghini & P. Engisch (Eds.), *A philosophy of recipes: Making, experiencing, and valuing* (pp. 199–214) Bloomsbury.

Ghabooli Dorafshan, S. M. H. (2021). Food with a taste of copyright: Feasibility of protecting culinary creations through artistic and literary law (comparative study of American and Iranian laws). *Private Law, 18*(2), 467–485.

Goldman, M. (2013). Cooking and copyright: When chefs and restaurateurs should receive copyright protection for recipes and aspects of their professional repertoires. *Seton Hall Journal Sports and Entertainment Law, 23*(1), Article 4.

29 Buffets v. Klinke

The previous two cases focused on whether copyright can protect recipes. This dispute looks at whether protection may be given by trade secret law.

Buffets Inc., a Minnesota company doing business as Old Country Buffets, ran a number of American budget buffet chain restaurants that served "all-you-can-eat" meals for a fixed price. In 1990, Buffets met the Klinkes, two successful restaurateurs, and gave them a tour of one of their restaurants. The Klinkes asked whether they could purchase a Buffets franchise, but Buffets was not a franchising outfit. In 1991, the Klinkes' son applied for a position as a cook at Buffets and was hired without ever disclosing his true residence or previous employment at his parents' company. He subsequently quit the Buffets after having gathered the necessary information to help his parents open a buffet restaurant.

Buffets alleged that the Klinkes obtained the recipes and manuals illegally and sued the Klinkes in the United States for misappropriation of trade secrets, specifically in relation to recipes for "simple American dishes," including barbecue chicken and macaroni and cheese, and work training manuals.

The US Court of Appeals eventually confirmed that the recipes and procedure manuals in question were standards of American cuisine and, in addition, they were basic, so that others may have known or discovered them independently; for that reason, they were not entitled to trade secret protection. The court also reasoned that the recipes had no economic value because "there was no demonstrated relationship between the lack of success of [the] competitors and the unavailability of the recipes." Buffets' cooks used simplified versions of the recipes in preparing their food and it was unlikely that the recipes themselves provided a benefit to Buffets. The court found that Buffets did not manage to establish that they derived any benefit from keeping the recipes secret and held that the recipes in question did not warrant trade secret protection.

The court also noted that the short tenure of Buffets' employees made it unreasonable for Buffets to complain when the manuals fell into the hands of rivals, especially when the company allowed its employees to keep the manuals without making them aware of their secrecy or taking adequate security measures to protect them. Following the manuals had more value than

DOI: 10.4324/9781003433675-35

keeping them confidential. As a result, the court dismissed Buffets' argument that the Klinkes had illegally obtained trade secrets.

Although Buffets took certain general protective measures, the court held that the company could not give evidence that reasonable measures to protect the confidentiality of the information in question had been adopted. It was hence concluded that general protective measures were inadequate, where employees were not informed of the trade secret status of manuals. While the Klinkes' acts to gain competitive advantage were unlawful and unethical, it was affirmed that the recipes and the manuals were not trade secrets.

This case is relevant to assess what is worthy of intellectual property (IP) protection within the operation of a restaurant business. The dispute shed light on the fact that at Buffets, emphasis was placed on food production rather than on the written recipe. Other restaurant operations, of course, may present different situations, where internal manuals and aspects such as the know-how related to tools and preparation techniques may convincingly be deemed worthy of IP protection.

Sources

BUFFETS, INC., a Minnesota corporation; and Evergreen Buffets, Inc., Court: United States Court of Appeals, Ninth Circuit, January 16, 1996, 73 F.3d 965 (9th Cir. 1996).

Diaz, P., & Rutherford, D. (1997). Restaurant espionage. *Cornell Hotel & Restaurant Administration Quarterly*, *38*(1), 43–50.

Saunders, K. M., & Flugge, V. (2020). Food for thought: Intellectual property protection for recipes and food designs. *Duke Law & Technology Review*, *19*(1), 159–197.

30 Magnolia Bakery
v. Apple Café

Magnolia Bakery opened its doors in 1996 in New York City's West Village. It expanded relatively quickly by opening branches throughout the United States and abroad, including Jordan, Mexico, the Philippines, Qatar, Saudi Arabia, and South Korea. Famously featured in television shows (most notably *Sex and the City*), movies (e.g., *The Devil Wears Prada*), and the media, the bakery is mostly known for its cupcakes.

Magnolia's cupcakes are iconic because of their icing, which makes them instantly recognizable: according to Magnolia, indeed, perfecting the signature swirl takes anywhere from 8 to 40 hours of practice. Magnolia keeps its cupcake formulas as trade secrets, including its "signature swirl." Accordingly, the company asks each of its bakers to sign confidentiality agreements, so as to safeguard its trade secrets as well as other intellectual or sensitive information.

In 2012, Magnolia sued one of its former employees in New York for allegedly stealing the bakery's signature swirl icing topping and sensitive, confidential information. According to Magnolia's lawsuit, the cupcakes sold by Apple Café presented the same swirled icing topping as Magnolia's unique and distinctive signature swirl. More specifically, Apple Café was accused of stealing Magnolia's cupcake recipes including breach of contract, trade secret theft, unfair competition, and tortious interference. It is interesting to note that in Magnolia's complaint it claimed confidentiality over a series of recipes, including:

> its black & white lemon, orange, caramel, banana and truffle cupcakes; white-out, coconut, lemon, caramel, banana, carrot, and flourless chocolate cakes; apple double crust, apple crumb, pumpkin, pecan, black bottom pecan, seasonal fruit, and fruit crisp pies; key lime and red velvet with a chocolate cookie crust cheesecakes; banana cream pie and blueberry jamboree ice box pies; strawberry and peppermint icebox cakes; cranberry chocolate chunk and whoopie cookies; whoopie pies; double fudge and pumpkin chocolate brownies; chocolate chunk blondie, and lemon peanut butter bars.

DOI: 10.4324/9781003433675-36

After the parties entered into a confidential non-disclosure agreement, the rival cupcake shop Apple Café closed its doors later that year.

Despite the fact that the lawsuit was promptly settled, it is not the first time Magnolia Bakery has sued one of its previous employees. The bakery also sued its co-founder, Jennifer Appel, alleging that as a consultant, she shared Magnolia's recipes and business secrets with Nicole Kotovos, who reportedly opened an unauthorized "Magnolia Bakery" in Greece. Nicole, on the other hand, claimed that her cupcake store was not even called "Magnolia Bakery," but rather "Hampton Cupcakes." Nonetheless, Magnolia Bakery obtained an injunction from a Greek court barring Nicole Kotovos from using the domain name "magnoliacupcakes.gr."

This case is particularly interesting in reflecting when intellectual property (IP) rights can be invoked on an artisanal product such as signature cupcakes. Magnolia Bakery's icing is arguably not among the most significant creative innovations in contemporary cuisine. At the same time, it provides a "dress" for a product that may be broadly comparable to that given to the Ferrero Rocher chocolate as acknowledged by the High Court of Delhi (Case 3 in this volume). Yet, while the latter was a dispute about the distinctiveness of a chocolate product's shape and packaging, the Magnolia Bakery case—as we have seen—focused on other IP infringements, particularly the misappropriation of trade secrets.

Sources

Appel, J., & Torey, A. (2009). *The Magnolia Bakery cookbook: Old fashioned recipes from New York's sweetest bakery.* Simon and Schuster.

Magnolia Intellectual Property, LLC v. Trawally *et al.* United States District Court for the Southern District of New York; 1:2012cv07102.

31 Masterpiece Cakeshop v. Colorado Civil Rights Commission

This case concerned a same-sex couple who went to a cakeshop in Lakewood, Colorado, in 2012 to order their wedding cake. The cakeshop owner, Jack Phillips, denied their order, claiming that he did not make cakes for gay couples' weddings due to his religious beliefs and because Colorado did not recognize same-sex marriage. Yet, Phillips did not prevent the couple from buying any baked goods from his store. As a result, the couple filed a complaint with the Colorado Civil Rights Commission about the cakeshop's discriminatory attitude toward the couple's sexual orientation.

The commission ruled in favor of the couple, ordering the cakeshop not to discriminate against same-sex couples by refusing to sell them wedding cakes or any other products that it would sell to heterosexual couples. The cakeshop chose to remove itself from the wedding cake business (which accounted for 40% of the total business revenue). The cakeshop's owner then appealed the decision, claiming that he did not want to comply with such an order, citing his freedom to choose his customers and religious beliefs, as well as his right of free speech.

The court of appeals upheld the decision, arguing that the nature of the cakeshop business is to comply with customer requests (which is expected of this kind of business) without imposing one's religious beliefs on one's customers and depriving same-sex couples of their rights under the Colorado anti-discrimination laws. The court confirmed that:

> it is a discriminatory practice and unlawful for a person, directly or indirectly, to refuse, withhold from, or deny to an individual or a group, because of disability, race, creed, color, sex, sexual orientation, marital status, national origin, or ancestry, the full and equal enjoyment of the goods, services, facilities, privileges, advantages, or accommodations of a place of public accommodation.

The case was then taken to the US Supreme Court, which declared in 2012 that the laws relating to same-sex marriage were unresolved, and that it was thus not unreasonable for the cakeshop to believe it was acting lawfully by

DOI: 10.4324/9781003433675-37

refusing service to the gay couple. The case had a mixed outcome, with the majority of the Supreme Court judges agreeing that anti-discrimination laws are not intended to interfere with religion, but that the laws apply equally to all businesses, prohibiting them from claiming religious beliefs when refusing their services or goods because same-sex couples should not be denied access to goods and services that heterosexual couples have access to.

Crucially, the Supreme Court's decision left open the key question of whether businesses that cannot refuse services to same-sex couples may in some instances incur violations of the religious rights or the rights to free speech of some of the parties involved. Three additional cases can help shed light on this question.

The first case took place between 2014 and 2018 in the United Kingdom, when Ashers Baking Company refused to make a cake with a message promoting same-sex marriage for Gareth Lee, a gay rights activist, citing the religious beliefs of Daniel and Amy McArthur, owners of the bakeshop. The UK Supreme Court ruled that Ashers was not committing direct discrimination toward Lee, as the McArthurs were acting based on their belief, citing the judgment of the US Supreme Court in Masterpiece Cakeshop v. Colorado Civil Rights Commission.

A second related dispute is Scardina v. Masterpiece Cakeshop, which took place subsequently and involved Masterpiece Cakeshop once again. In this case, the baker Jack Phillips initially agreed to make a birthday cake for a client named Autumn Scardina, but later refused to do so upon learning that the cake would have also celebrated a male-to-female gender transition. The Colorado Court of Appeals ruled that the act of refusal did not constitute a form of free speech, since "creating a pink cake with blue frosting is not inherently expressive and any message or symbolism it provides to an observer would not be attributed to the baker." The court also added that it is illegal to refuse to provide services to clients based on their race, religion, or sexual orientation.

Finally, a third related case is the US Supreme Court's decision in 303 Creative LLC v. Elenis, where it was held that a web designer could refuse to develop a website for a gay wedding invoking free speech rights. Notwithstanding the turnout of Scardina v. Masterpiece Cakeshop, 303 Creative LLC v. Elenis leaves open the door for future cases that wish to argue that growing, preparing, or sharing food may (in some specific instance) constitute an expressive act protected under free speech rights.

Sources

Detroit Timber & Lumber Co., 200 U.S. 321, 337. 303 CREATIVE LLC et al. v. ELENIS et al., June 30, 2023.

Laycock, D. (2019). The broader implications of Masterpiece Cakeshop. *Brigham Young University Law Review*, *1*, Article 7.

Lee v. Ashers Baking Company Ltd and others, October 10, 2018, UKSC 2017/0020 [2018] UKSC 49.
Masterpiece Cakeshop, Ltd., et al., Petitioners v. Colorado Civil Rights Commission, et al. 584 U.S., June 14, 2018, 138 S. Ct. 1719; 201 L. Ed. 2d 35.
Scardina v. Masterpiece Cakeshop, Inc., 528 P.3d 926, 2023 COA 8, January 26, 2023 (Colo. App. 2023).

Part VI
Boundaries

32 Basmati Rice

This is a dispute between India and Pakistan revolving around the protection of the name Basmati as a geographical indication (GI) in the European Union (EU). In September 2020, the EU published the 2018 India Protected Geographical Indication (PGI) application for Basmati. In the application it is stated that:

> "Basmati" is a special long grain aromatic rice grown and produced in a particular geographical region of the Indian sub-continent […]. The special characteristics of "Basmati" are its long slender kernels with a high length to breadth ratio, an exquisite aroma, sweet taste, soft texture, delicate curvature, intermediate amylose content, high integrity of grain on cooking, and linear kernel elongation with least breadth-wise swelling on cooking.

The production of the rice is restricted to a specific part of India. As stated in the application:

> [t]he area is a part in northern India, below the foothills of the Himalayas forming a part of the Indo-Gangetic Plains (IGP). In India, "Basmati" is grown and produced in all districts of the states of Punjab, Haryana, Delhi, Himachal Pradesh, Uttarakhand, as well as in specific districts of western Uttar Pradesh and Jammu & Kashmir.

If granted, the PGI status would suggest that India's Basmati rice is of certain quality, reputation, and characteristics based on its specific geographical origin. Indeed, such recognition would guarantee premium quality and the rice could fetch a higher price. In the application, India claims that there is a causal link between the above geographical area and the specific quality, reputation, and other characteristics of the rice in question. As specified in the application:

DOI: 10.4324/9781003433675-39

"Basmati" acquires its aroma, among other characteristics, as a result of the interplay of the longer light hours prevalent in the geographical area where it is grown, with other factors such as mild temperature during grain filling, humidity and solar radiation in the geographical area. [...] Taste and mouth feel characteristics are due to the prolonged sunshine in the longer days in the flowering months of "Basmati" in the geographic area. Ageing and pre-soaking of "Basmati" is known to enhance these characteristics.

Pakistan objected to this application, claiming that its farmers also produce high-quality Basmati rice. More specifically, the Rice Exporters Association of Pakistan filed a notice of opposition with the EU on behalf of Pakistan's farmers and exporters, who are at risk of losing billions of dollars of income. Pakistan argued that Basmati rice is a joint product of both India and Pakistan.

It is also interesting to note that there have been efforts in the past to file a joint India-Pakistan application, but such efforts have been fruitless.

Nepal also joined Pakistan in opposing India's Basmati application with the EU. It did so because Basmati is also traditionally grown and consumed in Nepal and is therefore part of the gastronomic culture of this country. Moreover, Nepal has frequently cooperated with scientists to develop different varieties of Basmati rice.

But the most bitter dispute is certainly between India and Pakistan. Historically, the EU has imposed zero tariffs on imported rice authenticated as genuine Basmati by either the Indian or Pakistani authorities. India's efforts to obtain GI protection for its rice was meant to discourage Pakistan's increasing exports of Basmati rice. India has even preceded Pakistan in protecting the name Basmati as a GI in its own territory (this happened in 2016). On the other hand, Pakistan enacted its GI legislation in March 2020, and it was not until early 2021 that it registered Basmati rice under its newly enacted GI legislation.

At the time of writing, the application is under examination. Both India and Pakistan are encouraged to negotiate and reach an amicable solution. If Pakistan's opposition fails, India will have the sole ownership of the Basmati GI in the EU.

The consequences of India prevailing in these opposition proceedings in the EU could be dire for Pakistani farmers and traders. Pakistan has a predominantly agrarian economy with agriculture accounting for roughly 25% of the gross domestic product and rice being the third-largest crop there in terms of growing area after wheat and cotton. Indeed, the impossibility for Pakistan to continue exporting Basmati-branded rice to a rich and vast market such as the EU would be a blow.

Sources

Biénabe, E., & Marie-Vivien, D. (2017). Institutionalizing geographical indications in southern countries: Lessons learned from Basmati and Rooibos. *World Development*, *98*(C), 58–67.

Marie-Vivien, D. (2008). From plant variety definition to geographical indication protection: A search for the link between Basmati rice and India/Pakistan. *The Journal of World Intellectual Property*, *11*(4), 321–344.

Rangnekar, D., & Kumar, S. (2010). Another look at Basmati: Genericity and the problems of a transborder geographical indication. *The Journal of World Intellectual Property*, *13*(2), 202–230.

Upreti, P. N. (2023). The battle for geographical indication protection of Basmati rice: A view from Nepal. *IIC-International Review of Intellectual Property and Competition Law*, *54*(5), 710–731.

33 Pisco

Pisco is a South American grape brandy that is typically colorless or yellow-ish amber in appearance. It is made in wine-making regions in Chile and Peru, and both countries claim it as their national drink. Both countries have strict pisco production regulations, but they are not identical. To reduce the alcohol content of pisco, Chile requires it to be diluted with water before it can be sold, whereas Peru prohibits any tampering. Moreover, Chilean pisco is made from fully fermented wine that is sometimes infused with fruit, giving it a yellow amber appearance, whereas Peruvian pisco is distilled from young wine, giving it a colorless look.

Historical political disputes between Peru and Chile that date back to 1929 (when the Treaty of Lima settled a long-standing territorial dispute and certain Peruvian territories passed to Chile) have contributed to various geographical indication (GI) battles between the two countries around the world. The term "pisco" has been protected as a GI in Chile for a long time, despite Pisco being a city and province in Peru (the origins of this spirit trace back to the mid-16th century when the Spanish took possession of what is now Peru and brought grapes that fit well with the sunny, arid grounds of the southern Peruvian city of Ica, which rose to prominence as Peru's birthplace of pisco). In India, the Peruvian government's application to protect pisco as a GI was challenged by Chile, but the name "Peruvian Pisco" was eventually confirmed as registered after nine years of battle. In Thailand, the dispute between Peru and Chile continues at the time of writing, with the local Registry of Industrial Property due to decide soon.

Chile has also scored some wins. For example, it has been successful in registering the designations Pisco and Chilean Pisco as GIs through bilateral trade agreements, including with the European Union (EU) (where pisco is protected as a Chilean Protected Designation of Origin (PDO)). Moreover, in 2006, Peru challenged Chile's trademark of Pisco Sotaqui (registered in Ecuador in 1994 and owned by Compañia Pisquera de Chile) before the Ecuadorian Trademark Office, claiming that the trademark was confusing consumers about the geographical origin of pisco. Peru lost this battle after five years. Furthermore, while Peru has registered pisco as a GI under the

DOI: 10.4324/9781003433675-40

Lisbon Agreement, some states which are party to this treaty have expressed their wish to refuse the protection of the Peruvian designation as they already protect Chile's right to sell Chilean Pisco.

A more balanced outcome was reached in the EU. In 2013, the Peruvian government registered pisco as an EU Protected Geographical Indication (PGI). According to the specifications, there are three categories of pisco distinguished by the kind of grape and level of fermentation: Pisco Acholado, Pisco Puro, and Pisco Mosto Verde. The designated area of production is bigger than the Peruvian city of Pisco, as it includes other provinces. The PGI application for pisco highlights how this product gets its specific quality and flavor from varying climatic and human factors:

> [t]he south coast of Peru, where the "pisco"-making area is located, is dry on account of marine currents, and the only natural humidity arises from the rare showers and mists which occur during winter. The low humidity and slight absence of precipitation during the year provide the best conditions for the grape, which once it is harvested will be of high quality and suitable for the production of the drink. The "pisco"-making area is characterised as having mixed soils (presence of clay, sandy and limy soil in equivalent proportions) and very sandy soils, with the water used for irrigation coming from river flooding, as these areas are to be found close to the foot of the Andes Mountain range. In this way the vineyards are irrigated with fresh water which helps to give better production and a high quality of grapes. To these elements must be added the growing practices used by the producer in their vineyards and the traditional method used to produce the product which owes its uniqueness to the combination of art, custom and valuable experience.

Yet, this PGI registration cannot prevent Chile's use of "pisco" in relation to drinks coming from Chile, because—as mentioned above—Chilean Pisco is protected as a PDO in the EU due to a bilateral agreement between Chile and the EU. Practically speaking, therefore, both nations can use the name "Pisco" and claim protection in the EU.

In terms of history, Peru appears to have a stronger standing due to its longer production across the centuries, but Chile currently produces more volume than Peru. If the conflict between Peru and Chile can be resolved and the two countries join forces in the spirits market, pisco may even be able to compete globally with more famous spirits.

Sources

Main Specifications of the technical file for "pisco" (EU Document 2011/C 141/16).

Mitchell, J. T., & Terry, W. C. (2011). Contesting pisco: Chile, Peru, and the politics of trade. *Geographical Review, 101*(4), 518–535.

Williams, P. B. F. (2022). The rise of geographical indications in Latin America: The case of pisco. In W. E. Murray, J. Overton, & K. Howson (Eds.), *Ethical value networks in international trade: Social justice, sustainability and provenance in the global south* (pp. 112–131). Edward Elgar.

34 Mānuka Honey

Long before mānuka became synonymous with mānuka honey, the Māori people regarded themselves to be the keepers of what they saw as a treasure. Mānuka honey is made by bees that feed on the pollen of the mānuka flower, which grows in both Australia and New Zealand. The honey is famous for its antibacterial effects, and both countries produce it, label it *mānuka*, and rely on that brand for securing multimillion-dollar exports. Certain mmānuka honey producers sell honey with a particularly high Unique Mānuka Factor rating for NZ$2,000–5,000 per jar. This factor is a grading system, and mānuka honey produced in New Zealand is eligible to obtain a UMF certificate. UMF stands for Unique Manuka Factor, the indicator of real mānuka honey from New Zealand.

The question of who can claim the name mānuka has sparked a battle between Australia and New Zealand. The Mānuka Honey Appellation Society of New Zealand applied to trademark the name in 2015, and the Intellectual Property (IP) Office of New Zealand eventually registered it in 2018. The trademark was opposed by the Australian Mānuka Honey Association claiming that the plant from which the honey is made, *Leptospermum scoparium*, is native to both countries. But the New Zealand Mānuka Honey Appellation Society argued that their mānuka honey is distinct from that of Australia, and that the Māori word "mānuka" has significant cultural significance in New Zealand and for New Zealand's First Nations peoples.

Australia has fostered the argument that the attempt to trademark the plant's name is illegal because there are numerous varieties of mānuka plants and that the plant also grows in Australia where it is generically called "tea tree." Paul Callander, chair of the Australian Mānuka Honey Association, stated that the anglicized word "mānuka" has been used in Australia since the 1930s and that the word has no meaning in the Māori language. He also claimed that the industry is uneven, with New Zealand dominating the market. Further, Australia invited New Zealand to work together on some protocols to share the name, to collaborate in the market, and to set the industry standards. New Zealand declined such a proposal.

DOI: 10.4324/9781003433675-41

After Australia lodged its objection, the Mānuka Charitable Trust (which was backed by NZ$6 million in government funding) was formed to represent the industry, iwi (tribes), and government and to advocate on New Zealand's behalf. Pita Tipene, its chair, stated that the goal was simple: to prevent the expression "mānuka honey" from being used on products made outside of New Zealand because the honey produced in New Zealand is made from mānuka trees. Furthermore, Tipene stated that New Zealand was the only country in the world to have adopted a scientific definition for mānuka honey, in regulations by the Ministry of Primary Industries.

But in 2023, the IP Office of New Zealand found that the opposition brought by the Australian Mānuka Honey Association was not grounded as the term in question was not distinctive enough to be a certification trade-mark—it would likely be deceptive and confuse consumers instead. While the ruling acknowledged that the Māori people first discovered the medical uses of this plant, it also conceded that when the trademark application was filed in 2015, Australians were already using the term "mānuka" to describe honey with antibacterial properties.

Sources

Finlay-Smits, S., Ryan, A., de Vries, J. R., & Turner, J. (2023). Chasing the honey money: Transparency, trust, and identity crafting in the Aotearoa New Zealand Mānuka honey sector. *Journal of Rural Studies, 100,* Article 103004.

Lloyd, P., Maclaren, D., Bardsley, P., & Lloyd, P. J. (2017). *Competition in the mānuka honey industry in New Zealand* (Working Paper No. 2033). Department of Economics, University of Melbourne.

Van Caenegem, W. (2017, May 28). The mānuka honey fight is one we have to have. *The Conversation.* https://theconversation.com/the-manuka-honey-fight-is-one-we -have-to-have-78261

35 Adan Krayan Rice and Rendang

Geographically adjacent, Indonesia and Malaysia share cultural practices, histories, and also cultural clashes. This has inevitably led to a number of disputes between the two countries, two of which are noteworthy. The first is over the use of a geographical indication, Adan Krayan, which refers to a type of rice grown in the Krayan area of Indonesia's North Kalimantan province. The other revolves around the claim of authenticity regarding a traditional dish: rendang.

The North Kalimantan region is well known for its wet rice cultivation, which produces white, red, and black rice types of high quality and taste. Yet, the Krayan region's large population is scattered over the Indonesian provinces of East and North Kalimantan, as well as across the border in the Malaysian states of Sabah and Sarawak on the Malaysian side of Borneo. In Indonesia, the rice is known as Adan Krayan rice, while in Malaysia the rice is known as Bario rice.

Back in 2012, Indonesia locally registered Adan Krayan rice as their geographical indicator (GI), which was enthusiastically welcomed by the press as a triumph against Malaysia, despite the fact that Malaysia had already registered Bario rice as its GI in 2008. According to the local press, Adan Krayan villagers were forced to sell their rice to the nearest towns in Malaysia due to Indonesia's geographical isolation and inadequate means of transportation to the main Indonesian cities. The indigenous peoples of the Krayan highlands and the Bario highlands (known as the Kelabit) are linguistically and culturally connected, and the national border has little impact on climate, altitude, and irrigation techniques used in rice farming.

Both the Indonesian and Malaysian governments appear to be hopeful about GI protection. Both GIs are now protected and continue to be used. However, the GI protection granted in Indonesia turns out to be of little use since appropriate transportation and market access issues to major Indonesian cities remain. Until road infrastructure is improved, the Adan Krayan people will be compelled to sell their rice to producers in Malaysia.

The legal standing of the dispute regarding rendang is different. This is a traditional food that originated with the Minangkabau people, commonly

DOI: 10.4324/9781003433675-42

known as "Minang," in the West Sumatra region of Indonesia's Sumatra Island. The recipe may have developed during the Portuguese occupation of Malacca in the 16th century, as they favored the use of spices from India.

A well-known traditional version of rendang uses beef as a central ingredient, although several variants are common too, including chicken, goat (possibly the earliest main ingredient of rendang), and oysters ("rendang lokan"). The recipe typically prescribes a long cooking time, as the term "rendang" comes indeed from "randang" or "merandang," which stand for "slowly." During preparation, the main ingredient (beef or one of its alternatives) is cooked with coconut milk, spices, lemongrass, ginger, shallots, chilies, and garlic.

Rendang is traditionally consumed during significant meals as a highly valued dish. Its history is inextricably linked to the actions of Minang traders who frequently traveled and passed between Sumatra and Malacca. Hence, the dish is entrenched with the Malay and Minangkabau cultures, and both peoples recognize it as part of their cultural heritage.

The rich entanglement of histories, cultures, and traditions makes rendang a prototypical culinary item for sparking disputes. To this, it should be added that rendang is an internationally renowned recipe: It is enjoyed by people of all socioeconomic classes and ethnic groups in Indonesia and Malaysia, and versions of rendang have traditionally existed in other countries too, including the Philippines and Singapore.

A diplomatic and mediatic dispute arose between Malaysia and Indonesia regarding claims of authenticity of rendang. The former claimed that the variants of rendang typical of Malaysia were distinct from those of Indonesia and, possibly, that the recipe originated from Malaysia (after all, the histories of Minang and Malaysian people are intertwined).

While no hard legal consequences have ensued so far, the dispute regarding the originality and identity of rendang stands as a textbook case of how nationalistic identity politics (i.e., a form of gastronationalism) is orthogonal to the rich and complex histories of recipes (a form of gastrodiplomacy).

Sources

Antons, C. (2017). Geographical indications, heritage, and decentralization policies: The case of Indonesia. In I. Calbory & W. L. Ng-Loy (Eds.), *Geographical indications at the crossroads of trade, development and culture: Focus on Asia-Pacific*. (pp. 485–507). Cambridge University Press.

Chong, J. W. (2012). "Mine, yours or ours?": The Indonesia-Malaysia disputes over shared cultural heritage. *Sojourn: Journal of Social Issues in Southeast Asia, 27*(1), 1–53. http://www.jstor.org/stable/43186922.

Fatimah, S., Syafrini, D., & Zainul, R. (2021). Rendang Lokan: History, symbol of cultural identity, and food adaptation of Minangkabau tribe in West Sumatra, Indonesia. *Journal of Ethnic Foods, 8*(1), 1–10.

Keating, S. (2018, June 11). How an outrage over crispy chicken united South-East Asia. *BBC.* https://www.bbc.com/travel/article/20180610-how-an-outrage-over-crispy-chicken-united-south-east-asia

Nurmufida, M., Wangrimen, G. H., Reinalta, R., & Leonardi, K. (2017). Rendang: The treasure of Minangkabau. *Journal of Ethnic Foods, 4*(4), 232–235.

36 Kimchi

The global demand for kimchi (also spelled *gimchi*, in accordance with the official Korean language romanization system adopted by South Korea) has been steadily rising since at least 2001, when the product was registered as Codex standard. Contextually, some Chinese companies established themselves as main actors in the international kimchi trade, including exports to South Korea. In fact, South Korea has a trade deficit with China when it comes to the kimchi trade.

As a result, a trade struggle ensued between China and South Korea. The first episode occurred in 2005 when a South Korean opposition leader alleged that Chinese-imported kimchi contained unsafe levels of lead. The Korean Food and Drug Administration (KFDA) rejected such a claim, stating that lead levels were lower and Chinese-imported kimchi was not harmful for human consumption. However, the KFDA declared that further investigations into Chinese-imported kimchi would be conducted due to an alleged parasitic insect egg contamination. China retaliated by claiming the same and stopped kimchi imports from South Korea into China. The disagreement was soon settled with a shared pledge to increase cooperation for hygiene and customs inspections.

A second important episode occurred in 2013. Among Chinese consumers, kimchi is usually referred to as "paocai" (or "Korean paocai"), a generic term that stands for all sorts of vegetables pickled in brine. To mark the distinctiveness of kimchi, in November 2013, the Korean government introduced an ad hoc term "xinqi," a composite word emerging from "xi" ("spicy") and "qi" ("unique"). A dispute then ensued at the diplomatic level as well as in the mass media and among lay people. Up for discussion was both the specific linguistic choice as well as the broader issue of whether the South Korean government has the right to advance requests over terms used to describe kimchi in other languages.

This linguistic dispute paralleled another feud over the habit of referring to kimchi with the expression "kimuchi" among Japanese speakers, which had its height in 2009 and 2010 when the girl band KARA used "kimuchi" during a television show.

DOI: 10.4324/9781003433675-43

The force with which South Korean institutions have intervened in these cases to guard kimchi identity is reminiscent of the 2006 effort sponsored by the Japanese government to certify the authenticity of Japanese cuisine abroad, and in particular sushi authenticity, at a time when sushi restaurants and sushi consumption had virally spread on a global scale. Labeled "sushi police" by its critics, the Japanese government initiative had relatively little impact.

These disputes attest to the growing soft power of South Korean culture and, at the same time, to the complexity of controlling its evolution on behalf of the South Korean government and institutions. While in 2013 UNESCO accepted South Korea's request to add "kimjang" (the tradition of making and sharing kimchi) to the Intangible Cultural Heritage list (see also Case 24 in this volume), kimchi itself is not a geographical indication and no international agreement besides the Codex regulates its process of production or the use of the term "kimchi."

In fact, kimchi has by now become a globally sought-after commodity and in the absence of a clearer framework concerning its cultural heritage and legal status, it is likely that future disputes will arise in international markets. Could kimchi be regarded as a sub-category of paocai, i.e., Korean paocai, from the perspective of a Chinese speaker and producer? While there may not be a clear argument to claim that kimchi is a generic term such as "feta," "pizza," or "sushi," some commentators of the linguistic disputes seem to suggest that kimchi producers in China or the United States (to name two major actors) may not need to abide by the standards envisaged by the South Korean government.

Sources

Chung, W. T. E. (2014). From "Paocai" to "Xinqi": The role of kimchi in Korean culinary nationalism and cultural identity. *Mercury - HKU Journal of Undergraduate Humanities*, *1*(1), 103–123.

Jang, D. J., Chung, K. R., Yang, H. J., Kim, K. S., & Kwon, D. Y. (2015). Discussion on the origin of kimchi, representative of Korean unique fermented vegetables. *Journal of Ethnic Foods*, *2*(3), 126–136.

Kyung-Koo, H. (2011). The "kimchi wars" in globalizing East Asia: Consuming class, gender, health, and national identity. In L. Kendall (Ed.), *Consuming Korean tradition in early and late modernity: Commodification, tourism, and performance* (pp. 149–166). University of Hawai'i Press.

Sakamoto, R., & Allen, M. (2011). There's something fishy about that sushi: How Japan Interprets the global sushi boom. *Japan Forum*, *23*(1), 99–121.

Surya, R., & Lee, A. G. Y. (2022). Exploring the philosophical values of kimchi and kimjang culture. *Journal of Ethnic Foods*, *9*(1), 1–14.

37 Rioja Wine

Rioja is a province in northern Spain well known for its wine production. The region has a long history of winemaking and has established a reputation for producing high-quality wines under the name "La Rioja." The wines produced in this region now enjoy Protected Designation of Origin (PDO) status in the European Union (EU) and in Spain protection as a collective trademark since 1925 and as a designation of origin since 1991.

The origin of wine production in La Rioja dates to ancient times, with a rich history spanning centuries. The region's winemaking tradition can be traced to the period when the Romans conquered the Iberian Peninsula. During Roman rule, the city of Calagurris (present-day Calahorra) in the region of La Rioja became an important hub for wine production. The Romans recognized the region's favorable climate and fertile soil, which provided ideal conditions for viticulture. They introduced advanced techniques and cultivated vineyards, laying the foundation for the wine industry in La Rioja. Following the decline of the Roman Empire, winemaking in La Rioja continued under Moorish and Christian rule. The presence of monasteries played a crucial role in preserving and advancing winemaking practices. Monastic orders such as the Cistercians planted vineyards and improved winemaking techniques, ensuring the continuity and quality of wine production.

Then, when Spanish explorers and settlers arrived in America for the first time, including in the territory that now encompasses Argentina, they often named places after towns or regions in Spain. This practice served to maintain a connection with their Spanish heritage and honor their places of origin. As a result, many cities, provinces, and regions in Argentina bear names that can be traced back to Spain. This is also the case of "La Rioja," a province in Argentina named by Juan Ramírez de Velasco, a Spanish citizen from Spanish Rioja, to pay homage to the place where he was born and raised. This area has a long winemaking tradition that began with the Spanish colonization.

Thus, there is an Argentine wine region, known as "La Rioja," which shares the same name as the Spanish wine region. As just mentioned, during the 19th century many Spanish individuals and families, including those from the Spanish Rioja, migrated to Argentina. These emigrants played a significant

DOI: 10.4324/9781003433675-44

role in shaping the foundation of modern winemaking in Argentina. Their influence had lasting impact, including adopting European toponyms or place names, which became deeply ingrained in the country's viticultural practices. Their use of European toponyms, in turn, influenced the state's decision-making process. As a result, laws and decrees were passed that standardized the use of European toponyms for Argentinean wine products. Argentina passed the Law on "Designation of Origin of Wines and Spirits" on September 15, 1999, and subsequently, in 2002, the term "La Rioja Argentina" was recognized as geographical indication (GI) in the South American country.

Yet, this geographical homonymity lays the ground for a clash of traditions. From a Spanish perspective, by using the term "La Rioja" Argentine winemakers usurped the prestige of the Rioja GI. More specifically, the use of this GI by Argentinean producers might confuse consumers, as they would associate the quality and reputation of the Argentinean wines with the Spanish wines. On the other side, Argentine winemakers vindicated the legitimacy of their tradition, as the geographical expression "La Rioja" refers to their region of production, too, attesting to a migration history that the EU itself had already recognized even before Spain joined the bloc and that ought not to be suppressed. In fact, rather than intending to mislead consumers, Argentine producers chose the label "La Rioja Argentina" to differentiate their wines from those originating from Spain.

The case was first examined by an administrative body in Argentina, which rejected the Spanish complaint. It was then brought before the Argentinean Federal Court, which dismissed it as well, in 2011. In its ruling, the Federal Court found that there was not sufficient evidence to prove that the labels could potentially confuse consumers, as the addition of the term "Argentina" in the geographical indication "La Rioja Argentina" clearly marked that only one of the two La Rioja wines is a product originating from the Argentinean Republic. Interestingly, the court further noted that because the designation "La Rioja Argentina" represents the name of the province from which the product originates, such designation ensures the fair treatment of producers and prevents consumer deception.

Sources

Bonadio, E., Contardi, M., & Lucchi N. (2024). *Geographical indications between the old world and the new world, and the impact of migration.* GRUR

Expediente N° 36.619/04 Caratulado "Consejo Regulador Denominación Origen Califica- da Rioja y Otro c/ E.N.- In. Vinicultura- Resol C32/02 y Otros/ Proceso de Conocimiento," decision of February 24, 2011.

Lechmere, A. (2011, May 4). Spain Loses "Rioja" name battle with Argentina. *Decanter.* https://www.decanter.com/wine-news/spain-loses-rioja-battle-with -argentina-39718/

38 Budweiser

The small city of České Budějovice is located in the South Bohemian region of the Czech Republic and has been known for centuries for the quality of its beer, which distinguishes itself in several elements including the high quality of the water of the nearby Vltava River as well as the use of Saaz hops from Žatec in northern Bohemia and of Moravian malted barley. For centuries, the city was a German-speaking enclave and played a significant political role during the Holy Roman Empire. For this reason, it was known also under its German name "Budweis" and its beer was referred to as "Budweiser," which in German literally means [beer] "from Budweis."

Brewing practices in use in České Budějovice can be traced back to the city origins in the 13th century. Over the course of centuries, practices diversified. A key moment was the establishment of a new town brewery in the 15th century. This brewery in fact specialized in producing "white" (wheat) beer, which distinguished itself in quality and reputation from the dark beers typically brewed locally. The brewery was later merged with another town brewery to form the Bürgerliches Brauhaus Budweis, or "civic brewery," which was owned and managed by the citizens of the town.

During the second half of the 19th century, the Czech-speaking population equaled and surpassed the German-speaking one. However, at the end of the 19th century, the management of "civic breweries" was still by and large under the control of German brewers. Thus, a Czech-owned brewery was founded in 1895 under the name "Český akciový pivovar" (in English: Czech Joint-Stock Brewery), which brought under one umbrella many small local Czech-owned breweries. Český akciový pivovar was eventually renamed Budějovický Budvar ("national corporation") and, to date, is the Czech Budweis producer.

This already rich history intertwines with another history of migration. After 1848, many Czechs moved to the United States. They started brewing beer overseas using the traditional knowledge accrued over centuries in their homeland, that is, according to the "Budweiser process," to deliver a product that was "similar in quality, color, flavor, and taste to the 'Budweiser' beer then being made in Bohemia." Thus, they used the name "Budweiser" to describe their beer.

DOI: 10.4324/9781003433675-45

A turning point in the Budweiser beer production in the United States occurred in 1876 when Anheuser & Company, a brewing company from St. Louis, Missouri, introduced a beer called "Budweiser." The company shortly after changed its name to Anheuser-Busch Companies Inc. and grew to become a key player in the global beer market. Anheuser-Busch has trademarked the name "Budweiser" in the United States (and several other countries) since 1886, and a second registration was obtained in 1907.

This paved the way for a long battle between the Czech brewer Budějovický Budvar and the US company Anheuser-Busch over the exclusive right to use the "Budweiser" name. In fact, the use of the name "Budweiser" to describe the beer produced in the United States seemed problematic to Budějovický Budvar, as the term itself means "from Budweis," which can be read as meaning "originating from Budweis." The Czech producer thus objected that the trademark registration and use by Anheuser-Busch was misleading and harmful to the reputation of its own products. Among other actions, Budějovický Budvar requested Protected Geographical Indication status in the European Union for Budweiser Budvar, which was granted in 2003.

The dispute led to a long sequel of agreements between Anheuser-Busch and Budějovický Budvar, starting from 1911. These contracts granted Anheuser-Busch the right to use the term "Budweiser" as a trademark worldwide, except for Europe, so long as it did not use the word "Original" in connection therewith. However, the Czech Budějovický Budvar still reserved the concurrent right to continue the use of the trademark and sell its "Budweiser" in the United States and throughout the world. Despite this, the agreement did not resolve the underlying issues, leading to a prolonged conflict that spanned several decades. A factor contributing to the breakdown of the truce is that, after World War II, the increased competition and market saturation in the American beer industry prompted Anheuser-Busch to seek new business prospects overseas—specifically in the United Kingdom, which was not yet part of the European Community at that time. The decision to engage in exportation resulted in a prolonged dispute between Anheuser-Busch and Budvar, which played out in various ways, including legal battles in the United Kingdom (by then a Member of the European Community), at (what is now) the Court of Justice of the European Union and in other European and non-European courts.

Sources

Bird, R. C. (2006). This bud's for you: Understanding international intellectual property law through the ongoing dispute over the Budweiser trademark. *Journal of Legal Studies Education, 23*, 53–85.

Calboli, I., & Ng-Loy, W. L. (Eds.). (2017). *Geographical indications at the crossroads of trade, development, and culture: Focus on Asia-Pacific*. Cambridge University Press.

Part VII

Biotechnology

39 GM Canola
Monsanto v. Schmeiser

This and the following case are about intellectual property rights owned by Monsanto, an American agrochemical company based in Missouri, which was acquired by Bayer in 2018. In 1993, the company had developed and patented a glyphosate-resistant gene for the canola plant, which makes canola resistant to the weed control product "Roundup." Monsanto sold the seed as Roundup Ready Canola and required farmers to enter into a formal agreement with Monsanto, which specified that new seed would have to be purchased every year.

Mr. Percy Schmeiser was a canola farmer who sprayed Roundup herbicide around power poles and canals adjacent to his land to destroy weeds. Schmeiser later noticed that some of the canola plants had survived and decided to conduct tests with Roundup. After applying Roundup to approximately three to four acres of land, Schmeiser noticed that more than half of the canola plants had survived. He then harvested the seeds and stored them separately from the rest of the harvest, allowing him to use it as seed for his one thousand acres of land.

At the time, Monsanto's canola seed was being utilized by many other farmers in the region, and when Monsanto discovered that Schmeiser was also cultivating Roundup-resistant canola crops, they approached him asking him to sign a patent licensing agreement and pay a license fee. Mr. Schmeiser refused to sign the agreement, claiming that he did not plant Roundup Ready Canola in 1997 and that his custom-bred canola crop fields had been accidentally polluted. Schmeiser further claimed that because the collected seeds were his physical property, he had the right to use it anyway he saw fit.

Monsanto then filed a patent infringement claim against Schmeiser with the Canadian Federal Court in 1998. The settlement discussions collapsed a year later, prompting Schmeiser to file a counterclaim against Monsanto for $10 million for libel, trespass, and polluting his crops. Despite the fact that there was extensive scientific proof as to how genetic alterations had been made, far more effort was spent on whether the seeds could have blown onto Schmeiser's land and accounted for what was growing on his fields in 1997.

DOI: 10.4324/9781003433675-47

The court ultimately ruled in favor of Monsanto, concluding that none of the sources mentioned by Schmeiser could explain the concentration or breadth of Monsanto's canola seeds on his fields. The court also upheld Monsanto's patent as valid and infringed. The ultimate ruling was upheld in 2002 by the Federal Court of Appeal, and subsequently in 2004 by the Supreme Court of Canada in a five to four ruling. The latter court did not put weight on the fortuitous contamination of Schmeiser's property when finding patent infringement. It concluded that "the general rule is that the defendant's intention is irrelevant to a finding of infringement. The issue is what the defendant does, not [...] what he intends." The case was also notable because the judges focused solely on patent infringement and ignored Schmeiser's concerns regarding biosafety and farmer rights.

This case was followed by two others on similar matters discussed in the US Supreme Court, which substantially aligned with the opinion in Monsanto v. Schmeiser. In Monsanto v. Geertson Seed Farms, Monsanto was granted the right to sell genetically modified alfalfa seeds to farmers and the latter the right to grow, harvest, and sell the product of such seeds. In Bowman v. Monsanto, farmers were denied the right to save and grow patented seeds without permission from the patent's owner. Jointly taken, Monsanto v. Schmeiser, Monsanto v. Geertson Seed Farms, and Bowman v. Monsanto constitute a formidable corpus of legal decisions that have exercised an influence over global food supply chains, besides dividing public opinion and institutions.

Sources

Busscher, N., Colombo, E. L., van der Ploeg, L., Gabella, J. I., & Leguizamón, A. (2020). Civil society challenges the global food system: The international Monsanto tribunal. *Globalizations, 17*(1), 16–30.

Monsanto Co., et al. v. Geertson Seed Farms, et al., June 21, 2010, 561 U.S. 139 (more) 130 S. Ct. 2743; 177 L. Ed. 2d 461.

Percy Schmeiser and Schmeiser Enterprises Limited v. Monsanto Canada Incorporated and Monsanto Company, May 21, 2004, 1 S.C.R. 902, 2004 SCC 34, 239 D.L.R. (4th) 271, 31 C.P.R. (4th) 161.

Robin, M. M., Smith, J. M., & Lasagna, M. (2008). *The world according to Monsanto.* Image & Compagnie.

Séralini, G. É., & Douzelet, J. (2021). *The Monsanto papers: Corruption of science and grievous harm to public health.* Simon and Schuster.

Vernon Hugh Bowman v. Monsanto Company, et al., March 19, 2013, 569 U.S. 278.

40 GM Seeds
Monsanto v. Nuziveedu

India has not been immune from high-profile biotech patent and plant variety litigations brought by Western multinationals. One of these disputes was Monsanto Technology LLC v. Nuziveedu & Ors. The US biotech company Monsanto owned a (now expired) patent protecting the process by which the gene Cry2Ab from the bacterium *Bacillus thuringiensis* is introduced into the cotton plant genome. The insertion of such a gene causes the plant to produce proteins that spare the crop from bollworm caterpillars. Many, if not most, Indian cotton-seed companies had accepted to pay a license fee or a trait fee to Monsanto to be able to introduce the gene into their varieties. However, Monsanto was requested to decrease the fee for Indian seed companies as part of a new price control policy introduced by the Indian government.

Then, in 2016, Monsanto began legal proceedings against Nuziveedu Seeds Limited at the Delhi High Court for alleged patent infringement. Nuziveedu, an Indian agritech company which markets seeds, had refused to pay Monsanto the additional sum requested by the US company in the context of their contractual relationship by invoking the above new policy—which pushed Monsanto to end the contract with Nuziveedu.

During the proceedings, Nuziveedu filed a counterclaim challenging the validity of Monsanto's patent. The patent was considered prima facie valid by the trial court. One of the main issues was whether the genetically engineered seed is excluded from the patentable subject matter under the Indian Patent Act. Pursuant to this law, a gene occurring in nature is not patentable. Specifically, the Indian Patent Act excludes from patentability:

> plants and animals in whole or any part thereof other than micro-organisms but including seeds, varieties and species and essentially biological processes for production or propagation of plants and animals.

Since a considerable amount of skill is involved in identifying the function, location, and isolation of a gene, the question arose whether such isolated genes are in fact patentable. In particular, Monsanto was pushing the argument that the nucleotide acid sequence which contains the gene Cry2Ab was

DOI: 10.4324/9781003433675-48

a patentable microorganism. The Delhi court did not agree on this and eventually revoked the patent.

The issue inevitably turned political, as Monsanto has a record of going after farmers for technology infringement with lawsuits or threats thereof. Ultimately, the patentability aspect of the case was settled but, needless to say, the legal suit by the US multinational enterprise sparked vivid criticism among many sectors of Indian society that resulted in the development of domestic legal activism to support Nuziveedu Seeds in this legal battle, with insiders hoping to reach a result similar to the one obtained by a coalition of opponents, supported by the Indian government, in the famous neem tree biopiracy case at the European Patent Office.

While this case concerns cotton, the dispute is of significance to Indian farmers growing plants and agricultural products for food production as well. In the end, according to several commentators, the settlement has endangered the integrity of the Indian Patent Act. In fact, even though the government prohibits seed patents and trait fees, farmers will continue to pay the fees for patents on seeds based on the private agreements between farmers and patent holders.

Sources

Monsanto Technology LLC v. Nuziveedu and Ors. AIR 2019 SC 559.

Peschard, K., & Randeria, S. (2020). Taking Monsanto to court: Legal activism around intellectual property in Brazil and India. *The Journal of Peasant Studies, 47*(4), 792–819.

41 Heme

This is a still pending (at the time of writing) legal fight between two competitors in the plant-based meat industry, i.e., the US companies Impossible Foods (based in Boston) and Motif Foodworks (based in California). The case focuses on the use of heme protein meat alternatives which give a deep red color and meaty flavors to plant-based burgers and similar products. Differently from other competitors in the alternative protein market, Impossible Foods' products include "heme." This molecule can be found in nature (including in animals, where it serves the function of being a precursor to hemoglobin) and makes the blood red, contributing to bringing oxygen to the body. It is abundant in animal muscle tissue, occurs naturally in all living organisms, and is identical to the heme molecule found in normal meat.

   Impossible Foods argues that its researchers discovered that heme is crucial for the aroma, taste, and mouthfeel of animal-derived meat. Specifically, the company claims that adding soy leghemoglobin to its products gives them such features—this is a compound that is found in nature in the root nodules of soybean plants. And Impossible Foods has obtained patents in a number of countries covering heme-related methods and materials. For example, the US patent for "Methods and compositions for consumables" refers to:

> improved methods and compositions which more accurately replicate the characteristics that consumers value in the preparation and consumption of meat and which overcome the shortcomings and drawbacks of current meat substitutes.

Interestingly, Impossible Foods' CEO Patrick Brown is listed as co-inventor of this patent. Another US patent owned by Impossible Foods, "Ground meat replicas," refers to:

> plant-based products that mimic the texture, appearance, and sensory aspects of ground meat, including the texture, appearance, and sensory aspects of cooking and eating ground meat, such as the fibrousness, heterogeneity in texture, beefy flavor, and red-to-brown color transition during

DOI: 10.4324/9781003433675-49

cooking of ground meat. This disclosure also relates to compositions and methods for altering the flavor of a food product or a food replica, such as a cheese or meat replica.

In late 2021, the California-based Motif Foodworks—a 2019 spinout of the biotech company Ginko Bioworks—launched its own Hemami ingredient that recreates the heme naturally found in animal meat and began using biotech techniques and other innovative processes to produce ingredients for plant-based meat, eggs, and dairy which could mimic the real products. Impossible Foods was not happy about a competitor exploiting (what they consider) new techniques and in March 2022 sued Motif on patent infringement grounds before the US District Court of Delaware. Impossible Foods claims that Motif infringed its patent rights in connection with the use of heme to recreate certain features of real animal meat in plant-based alternatives. They also made the point that Motif was willfully violating their patent rights, which could increase the amount of compensation the company would be entitled to if the Delaware court finds the case to be one of patent infringement. Impossible Foods has also asked for an injunction order against Motif which—if granted—would block their manufacture and sale of any meat substitute containing Hemami.

On the other hand, Motif defended the case by stating that many of the features claimed in Impossible Foods' patents are obvious and already disclosed in the prior art. That is also why they asked for the cancellation of several heme-based patents owned by Impossible Foods, especially in the United States and Europe. One of these opposition proceedings was actually successful and in November 2022 the Opposition Division of the European Patent Office (EPO) revoked a patent held by Impossible Foods. Indeed, the EPO sided with Motif holding that the invention in question was obvious also considering that the ingredients used to develop the taste and smell of meat and meat alternatives in food products have been known for decades. Moreover, Motif has asked for and obtained an inter partes review of another US patent owned by Impossible Foods, which covers "food products containing highly conjugated heterocyclic rings complexed to an iron ion and one or more flavor precursors, and using such food products to modulate the flavor and/or aroma profile of other foods."

Motif also launched a public awareness campaign portraying Impossible Foods as a bully wishing to curtail competition in the alternative protein market. The dispute is being followed closely by stakeholders in the plant-based industry, especially by other competitors concerned about the scope of protection of Impossible Foods' patents, which could effectively prevent anyone in the market from using heme proteins for meat substitutes.

Sources

Poinski, M. (2023, June 21). Impossible foods' heme patent will be reviewed in dispute with motif food works. *Food Dive.* https://www.fooddive.com/news/impossible-foods-heme-patent-reviewed-motif-foodworks/653387/

Ground Meat Replicas, US patent 10798958B2, Inventors Ranjani Varadan, Sergey Solomatin, Celeste Holz-Schietinger, Elysia P. Cohn, Ariel Klapholz-Brown, Jennifer Woan-Yi Shiu, Aniket KALE, Jessica Karr, Rachel Fraser. https://patents.google.com/patent/US10798958B2/enhttps://patents.google.com/patent/US10798958B2/en

Methods and Compositions for Affecting the Flavor and Aroma Profile of Consumables, US patent 9700067B2, Inventors Rachel Fraser, Patrick O'reilly Brown, Jessica Karr, Celeste Holz-Schietinger, Elysia Cohn. https://patents.google.com/patent/US9700067B2/en

Methods and Compositions for Consumables, US patent 10863761B2, Inventors Patrick O'reilly Brown, Marija Vrljic, Ranjani Varadan, Michael Eisen and Sergey Solomatin, Current Assignee Impossible Foods Inc. https://patents.google.com/patent/US10863761B2/en

42 Essentially Biological Tomatoes and Broccoli

In European patent law, a process is essential biological if it consists entirely of natural phenomena such as crossing or selection. For example, as clarified by the European Patent Office (EPO) itself, a process for the production of plants or animals that is based on the sexual crossing of whole genomes and on the subsequent selection of plants or animals is excluded from patentability as being essentially biological. Several patent laws around the world, including in Europe, consider essentially biological processes unpatentable—and they do so because they treat processes and laws of nature as already occurring in nature and therefore not monopolizable.

The disputes in question stem from two patents issued by the EPO in November 2003. The tomato patent was granted to the State of Israel (Ministry of Agriculture) and was challenged at the EPO by Unilever. The broccoli patent was granted to the British company Plant Bioscience and opposed by two competitors, Syngenta Participations AG and Groupe Limagrain Holding. The two cases were then referred to the EPO's Enlarged Board of Appeals (EBA), the EPO's highest board to which the most important cases are referred and which has the task of guaranteeing the uniform application of European patent law. The two disputes were then consolidated. In March 2015, the European Patent Office ruled that plants or seeds obtained through essentially biological processes should be considered patentable.

The tomato patent protected a "method for breeding tomatoes having reduced water content and product of the method" predominantly including steps of conventional breeding techniques of crossing and selection (e.g., the fruit is allowed to remain on the vine past the point of normal ripening in order to be screened and selected for increased dry weight percentage). The broccoli patent covered a "method for selective increase of the anticarcinogenic glucosinolates in brassica species" involving the crossing and selecting of plants, and a further technical feature consisting of checking for molecular markers in the broccoli. Thus, both cases involved processes for producing plants not using sophisticated genetic engineering but just traditional breeding techniques. They are an example of a new type of innovative plant developed via conventional breeding methods, so-called "native traits." It should

DOI: 10.4324/9781003433675-50

be remembered that the agrotechnology industry does not neglect such traditional techniques, knowing there is a share of consumers who strongly dislike genetically modified organisms and instead prefer traditional techniques based on crossing and selecting.

So, in both the tomato and broccoli cases the EBA found that plant products such as seeds, fruits, and parts of plants can be patented even where they are obtained through essentially biological breeding methods involving crossing and selection. It also clarified that the exclusion of essentially biological processes for the production of plants does not extend to a patent claim for a product that is directly obtained from or defined by such a breeding process. The bottom line being that plants or seeds generated by conventional breeding methods were considered patentable here.

As was to be expected, the plant industry lauded the EBA's decision, whereas the reaction from civil society was strongly negative. Grassroots organizations focusing on biodiversity conservation did not hesitate to affirm that the EPO aimed at pleasing agribiotech corporations such as Syngenta and Monsanto to the detriment of farmers, small breeders, and final consumers. The risk they highlight is that an increased monopolization of food plants with proprietary rights being consolidated in the hands of few companies can jeopardize food production and biodiversity. As noted by "No Patents on Seeds," a grassroots group, there are concerns that "patents on plant and animal breeding will foster further market concentration, erode small breeding companies, making farmers and other stakeholders of the food supply chain even more dependent on just a few big international companies and ultimately reduce consumer choice."

As mentioned, this decision is widely considered controversial. It is probably for this reason that in a subsequent case—i.e., Peppers—the EPO was bold enough to reverse such a position. The next case summary concerns that dispute.

Sources

G2/12 (Tomato II) and G2/13 (Broccoli II), March 25, 2015.

Minssen, T., & Nordberg, A. (2015). The impact of "Broccoli II" and "Tomatoes II" on European patents in conventional breeding, GMOs, and synthetic biology: The grand finale of a juicy patents tale? *Biotechnology Law Report, 34*(3), 81–98.

State of Israel - Ministry of Agriculture v. Unilever N.V. & Plant Bioscience Limited v. Syngenta, 25 March, 2015. *ECLI:EP:BA:2015:G000212.20150325.*

European Patent Office upholds patents on broccoli and tomato - Patents on plants and animals derived from conventional breeding can also be granted in future, No Patents on Seeds, 27 March, 2015. https://www.no-patents-on-seeds.org/en/node /302

43 Essentially Biological Peppers

As we have just seen, the tomato and broccoli patents were criticized because legal monopolies were given over plants obtained via essentially biological processes.

The decision by the European Patent Office (EPO) Enlarged Board of Appeal (EBA) in those cases has also left the European Union (EU) disappointed. After the tomato and broccoli ruling, the European Parliament asked the European Commission to review the rules on the patentability of plants and animals obtained from essentially biological processes. The Commission reviewed them and reiterated the point that plants and animals generated by these processes, or parts thereof, should be excluded from patentability. Moreover, several European states including Belgium, France, and the Netherlands amended their own patent laws to explicitly make them unpatentable. Not only did the EU took action to oppose that position. The EPO itself modified its own implementing regulations, clarifying that patents cannot be given for plants or animals exclusively obtained through an essentially biological process.

The EBA had the chance to come back to this thorny issue in the pepper case. The dispute came from a European patent application filed by the Swiss giant Syngenta Participations AG for an invention entitled "New pepper plants and fruits with improved nutritional value." In May 2020, the EBA released its opinion interpreting the rule which excludes essentially biological processes from patentability. It did so after considering 41 amicus curiae briefs from a variety of organizations, law firms, and corporations.

The EBA gave what it called a "dynamic interpretation" of the legal provision in question, affirming that the non-patentability of essentially biological processes extends to plant and animal products that are exclusively obtained through such processes. Consequently, this is a complete reversal of the 2015 EBA tomato and broccoli decisions, meaning that plants obtained by traditional breeding steps, e.g., mixing genes of the parental lines, cannot be patented anymore in Europe.

But this does not mean that patents cannot be granted in relation to breeding techniques that incorporate a technical step. Technologies that increase

DOI: 10.4324/9781003433675-51

the productivity of plants or animals or improve the steps of crossing or selection involved in classical breeding, e.g., by introducing a trait into the genome or modifying a trait of the genome of the plant, can still be patented. In other words, if the process does not consist of a mere sexual crossing of plants, patents should still be available. Yet, as we have seen, after the pepper decision it is no longer possible to obtain patents claiming plants or plant products in Europe should the new trait be the outcome of traditional crossing and selection alone without a further step of a technical effect.

This is certainly not good for the agribiotech industry as innovators in this field always expect to recoup their investments via obtaining and enforcing patents protecting the outcome of their research. Concerns have also been raised over possible political motivations behind the EBA ruling in the pepper case. For example, Jörg Thomaier, director of the intellectual property department at Bayer, stated:

[a]s a company, we are disappointed by the decision. Of course, it is the task of a court to decide the one way or the other, but I am concerned that the decision seems to be politically driven. [...] The decision will hamper future agricultural patent innovation[s], which are needed to overcome the challenges in agriculture.

The voice from the civil society is the opposite, though. Grassroots organizations, farmers, and other pressure groups note that the developers of the pepper invention did not invent anything new. What they did—the argument goes—was just to take advantage of a completely biological process, which already existed in nature, with the intention of monopolizing the fruits of such a process. According to the environmental group Friends of the Earth:

[f]or more than ten years we have been fighting against patents such as those on broccoli, tomatoes, peppers, melons and cereals. Therefore, we welcome this verdict in the name of the European public, gardeners, farmers and consumers. Knowledge of methods of breeding plants and animals continues to evolve as a common good from the activities of farmers and breeders over centuries, it is not invented by industry. In future, conventionally bred plants and animals have to be kept available for further breeding.

Sources

G3/19, Pepper (follow-up to "Tomatoes II" and "Broccoli II"), May 14, 2020.
Riemenschneider, P. L. (2021). Who owns the pepper? *Stockholm Intellectual Property Law Review*, *1*, 18–27.

Part VIII
Empowerment

44 Red Bush Tea[1]

As mentioned, geographical indication protection status is given to products whose quality is strictly linked to a local area and peculiar manufacturing techniques. In 2021, the European Union (EU) added the South African rooibos (red bush) tea to its Protected Designation of Origin (PDO) register. This iconic tea was the first African product to receive this status in the EU and at that time the 40th from a non-EU country. There are hopes that the designation will contribute to the product's global standing and that this will have benefits for the region.

Rooibos is obtained through the infusion of dried leaves or stems of *Aspalathus linearis*. The plant grows in Cederberg, a mountain region with fertile soil north of Cape Town, and in harsh microclimate conditions with hot dry summers and wet winters. The bushy plant is grown following a specific process to produce a tea that is fruity, woody, spicy in taste, and naturally caffeine free. The use of the dried leaves and stems of rooibos as a tea was first reported in 1772, although Khoisan indigenous people from western South Africa have been consuming a drink made with rooibos for centuries. The name itself derives from the Afrikaans language, meaning "red bush" and referring to the plant's red-brown leaves.

The South African government has hailed the EU PDO status for rooibos. According to the Minister of Agriculture, the new EU status will "signal its unique quality to consumers, not only in Europe but all over the world." Such legal protection thus matters, also considering that attempts at misappropriation of the rooibos brand have occurred in the past. In 2013, for example, a French company tried to register the trademark "rooibos" for skincare products in France (one of the health benefits of this tea is its rich antioxidant content which may improve skin health).

It is hoped that the EU designation will offer rooibos producers and farmers a valuable market advantage, because only infusions produced in the local area north of Cape Town and according to specific rules can now be labeled "rooibos."

---

1 This summary is based on an article authored by Enrico Bonadio and Magali Contardi entitled "Rooibos tea: EU protection is good news for South African agriculture," published in *The Conversation* on June 29, 2021.

DOI: 10.4324/9781003433675-53

This ensures that tea produced in other areas cannot be sold in the EU—one of the biggest markets in the world—under the name rooibos or red bush. Evocative uses of such designations by third parties (for example, "Rooibos kind," "Red Bush type," "Rooibos style," or "Red Bush imitation") are also prohibited.

It is also hoped that this kind of brand monopoly in a very important market like the EU will enhance the economic development of the whole of South Africa. The region already produces an average of 14,000 tons of rooibos per year, and in 2019/20 expanding global demand resulted in an increase to about 20,000 tons.

The South African Rooibos Council estimated that total rooibos sales in 2020 equaled six billion cups of tea—close to one cup per human on Earth. It also reported that half the production is consumed locally, whereas the other half is exported to more than 60 countries. In 2019, the biggest export markets were Germany (28%), Japan (22%), the Netherlands (9%), and the United Kingdom (8%).

The global herbal tea market is growing at 7% per year. With rooibos' new EU status, not only is the global demand for this product expected to increase; related sectors, such as agritourism, are also likely to benefit. In 2021, an EU report revealed that European food products listed on the EU register of all protected geographical names generated an estimated sales value of €77 billion in 2017, suggesting potential positive effects on non-European products listed in the EU register as well.

As the example of Darjeeling tea shows, premium pricing and more robust revenues often follow geographical name protection because of consumer recognition of the product's quality. This is exactly what farmers and the entity that manages the rooibos brand (the South African Rooibos Council) now expect. The rooibos EU designation could also contribute to further promoting South African gastronomic heritage and genetic resources. As Mogale Sebopetsa, head of the Western Cape Department of Agriculture, explained, "in this way, we safeguard our heritage for posterity." Employment could be boosted, too. As confirmed in the rooibos council report, the rooibos industry is already the biggest employer of people from the rural provinces of South Africa, with direct income and employment given to more than 8,000 farm workers, and many others in the supply chain (processing, packaging, retailing). With more production and international sales in sight, this trend will probably increase.

Sources

Troskie, D., Biénabe, E., & Swart, M. (2022, July). "Rooibos"/"red bush": The first African GI included in the EU register. *Worldwide perspectives on geographical indications. Centre de Coopération Internationale en Recherche Agronomique pour le Développement [Cirad], Montpellier, France.* https://hal.science/hal-03791361

45 Madd de Casamance

Madd is a species of wild tropical plants that bear large (up to 8–10 cm) and fragrant berries. With their orange-yellow skin when mature, these fruits are high in carbohydrates as well as vitamins (A, K, and C), and they are commonly used in the production of juice, syrup, and preserves. Plant specimens grow predominantly in the woodlands and in some savannahs of West Africa, including Burkina Faso, Senegal, Guinea, Guinea Bissau, Mali, Ghana, and Côte d'Ivoire. Madd consumption is to date a practice that builds on traditional forms of community sustenance and sustainable forms of forest use.

The Southern Senegal's Casamance region is especially well known for its production of madd fruits, which are praised for their flavor and medicinal properties. The production is distinctive not only because of its sustainable use of forest resources but also in terms of the role that local women have taken in shaping it. In fact, thanks also to the collaboration with the Economie Territoires et Développement Services (ETDS), a Senegalese non-governmental organization, women from Casamance play a key role in processing and selling madd fruits harvested in the region, notably in Dakar.

Discussions about the opportunity to register the name "Madd de Casamance" as a geographical indication (GI) began in 2017 with a subregional conference organized by the Food and Agriculture Organization of the United Nations and the World Intellectual Property Organization in collaboration with the Organisation Africaine de la Propriété Intellectuelle (OAPI) and the Senegalese Agency of Industrial Property and Innovation. Local farmers themselves expressed their desire to protect this name in several countries. These efforts culminated in the establishment of the Association pour la Protection et la Promotion de l'Indication Géographique Madd de Casamance (APPIGMAC), whose purpose is to bring together all those involved in the region's fruit harvesting, processing, and distribution. APPIGMAC is also involved in the protection and promotion of Madd de Casamance and its products. It has allowed local producers to exchange ideas and agree on standard procedures for managing their quality assurance processes, which are required to ensure that the fruits meet required specifications. APPIGMAC is also looking for new markets and programs to boost value and sales.

DOI: 10.4324/9781003433675-54

Madd de Casamance represents an important example of how GIs can help with the environmental, social, and economic components of sustainability and the transition to a green future. As a group effort, if protection is obtained, it has the potential to boost efforts in Senegal to scale up ecologically friendly practices that would otherwise be more difficult to achieve by individual companies. More broadly, the Madd de Casamance brand has the potential to become the region's showcase GI and, if finally granted, Africa's first GI for a wild product.

While the granting of this GI would plausibly mark a positive turnout from the point of view of environmental, social, and food justice, it should also be approached with caution. Product renown often comes at the cost of its integrity, as it threatens to disrupt sustainability of production both from an ecological point of view (this is especially true since madd is a fruit harvested in the wild) and from a socio-economic perspective, given the chief role that women have had so far in leading the production system.

Sources

Avena, A. W. (2022, July). Geographical indications as the engine of traditional communities rights. *Worldwide perspectives on geographical indications. Centre de Coopération Internationale en Recherche Agronomique pour le Développement [Cirad], Montpellier, France.* https://hal.science/hal-03791870/document

Kanoute, P. T. (2020). Supporting environmental sustainability with GIs: The case of "Madd de Casamance". *WIPO MAGAZINE, 2*, 36–42.

46 Cabrito de Tete

Cabrito de Tete is goat meat from the Tete area of Mozambique. The province of Tete has a goat population of around 300,000, which has increased over the last decades. The high quality of this meat is due to a combination of the feeding of the animal itself (it feeds on natural pastures, consisting especially of dry grass and malambe) and the geographical characteristics of the Tete region, with its distinctive tropical and dry climate. Due to these circumstances the meat's flavor is sweet and persistent, with a mild aroma and soft texture—and it can also boast low caloric and cholesterol levels.

In June 2020, the term "Cabrito de Tete" was registered as a geographical indication (GI) in Mozambique. It is the first GI in this country and the first for a member state of the African Regional Intellectual Property Organization (ARIPO), to which 17 African states belong. ARIPO is a regional inter-governmental organization which facilitates cooperation among certain (mainly anglophone) African states in intellectual property matters. The GI registration of Cabrito de Tete is the result of a long preparatory process, which—Mozambique's authorities hope—will lead to additional intellectual property protection, new business chances, and high-quality products.

The owner of the GI is the Associação para a Protecção e Promoção do Cabrito de Tete, the entity that manages and supervises the production and sale of the goats. The designated areas of production are the southern region of Tete Province and some nearby regions with identical climatic conditions. In these areas, goat feeding and management are different from those practiced in the interior and northern regions of the province. Thus, strict standards apply to the breeding and processing of Cabrito de Tete—the aim being the preservation of the reputation of the local goat meat and the protection of its producers.

Cabrito de Tete is also the first African GI product that is not predominantly manufactured by Arabs (as is the case with Argan oil which received GI status in Morocco in 2010) or white Europeans (this is the case of Rooibos tea, which as we have seen is registered as a Protected Designation of Origin in the European Union (EU)). The hope is that GI protection of the Tete goat in the African market gradually facilitates the penetration of the product on

DOI: 10.4324/9781003433675-55

the continent. It would be a success for the rural sector of the Tete area and Mozambique more broadly.

Interestingly enough, this registration was supported by the EU Intellectual Property Office and AfrIPI, an international cooperation project funded and directed by the EU. The EU Ambassador to Mozambique, Antonio Sanchez-Benedito Gaspar, pointed out:

> [t]he European Union is pleased to share with Mozambique its vast experience in adopting geographical indications. We congratulate the Government for the commercial launch of CABRITO DE TETE, the first Mozambican product to have obtained such a standard. It is also an important means of working very closely with rural producers, to establish sustainable and specific means of production which confers them the geographical indicator label.

Yet, concerns have also been raised, in particular with regard to the environmental impact of the GI. Like other ruminants including sheep and cows, goats produce methane (a potent greenhouse gas) in two ways: via their digestion process and via their waste. It was pointed out that the Cabrito de Tete GI could lead to a fast and high increase in goat breeding, which in turn would lead to an increase in greenhouse gas emissions in the production area, with a negative impact on the health of the local people, animals, plants, and ecosystems.

Others have voiced the opposite opinion, though. It has been argued that the contribution of goats to rural communities in Mozambique is important for food security (direct consumption of meat); resilience to shocks, employing goats as savings and insurance; income generation from the sale of meat, skins, and other related products; and the cultural and social connections, where goats are used at birthdays, weddings, religious ceremonies, and other social events. Also, because of their nutritional and climatic adaptability, goats contain protein and have an enhanced ability to survive in many of the most inhospitable areas of the plain, predominantly because of their resistance to heat.

Sources

Upreti, P. N. (2023). *Geographical indication protection of Mozambique's Cabrito de Tete (Tete Goat)*. Report of the United Nations Conference on Trade and Development, UNCTAD/ALDC/2023/1. http://creativecommons.org/licenses/by /3.0/igo/

47 Sugarloaf Pineapple

In October 2021, Benin registered its first protected geographical indcation (GI) with the Organisation Africaine de la Propriété Intellectuelle (OAMI). OAMI is a regional intellectual property organization whose 17 member states are mostly French-speaking countries. The protected name is Ananas Pain de Sucre du Plateau d'Allada (Sugarloaf pineapple from the Allada Plateau). The fruit is cultivated predominantly in South and Central Benin, with 83% of the production coming from the Allada Plateau in the south of the country. The Sugarloaf pineapple has delicious and sweet white flesh, with the distinction of remaining green until completely mature.

The recognition of the Sugarloaf pineapple as a GI came after several years of negotiations between the government of Benin, industry stakeholders, the European Union, and the French Development Agency, with additional guidance from the Food and Agriculture Organization (FAO). In fact, the Benin government has devoted special attention to the pineapple sector, which—together with cotton and cashew nuts—is one of the crops with the strongest export potential. It is hoped that this GI protection will help preserve and promote this precious part of Benin's agriculture sector, retaining or advancing the farmers' know-how while protecting it; in the words of Sibylle Slattery, project coordinator in the FAO Food and Nutrition division:

> [i]t is a very long process, but Geographical Indications represent a real tool for development and, if they are successful, they can bring value to the whole food value chain, including smallholders.

It is believed that the Sugarloaf pineapple GI will contribute to rural development in African countries and help position African products on regional, continental, and international markets. It is one of the earliest and clearest examples of how GIs can be a tool to empower consortia of producers in countries that struggle to gain commercial and market visibility. The case attests that GIs can serve to advance issues of social, economic, and environmental justice in some circumstances. While soft tools of distinction—such as the Slow Food Ark of Taste project—show promise, the international legal

DOI: 10.4324/9781003433675-56

recognition of GIs conveys value and robustness to consortia. This, of course, only if a coordinated support at multiple institutional levels exists.

Overall, the GI will likely add value to Sugarloaf pineapples and improve the income from the export sales. According to the *Economist*:

> what ham is to Parma, cheese is to Caerphilly and sparkling wine is to a certain region of France, the spiky-haired sugarloaf pineapple is to Benin.

At the same time, GI recognition also poses some challenges. One of which is for producers, who must keep up with the GI requirements (particularly the quality and consistency of supply) if they wish to hold on to the GI recognition. A different challenge, instead, regards the achievement of a viable balance between profitability and sustainability. While GI status may drive an increase in market demand for Sugarloaf pineapples, the historical trajectories of other GIs show the need to carefully manage natural and social resources that undergird production.

Sources

Fadinaa, A. M. R., & Barjolleb, D. (2018, July 1–5). *Geographical indications to enhance the value chain of agricultural and agri-food products in Benin: Sugar loaf pineapple and Wagashi case.* 13th European International Farming Systems Association (IFSA) Symposium, Farming Systems: Facing Uncertainties and Enhancing Opportunities (pp. 1–13). International Farming Systems Association (IFSA) Europe, Chania, Crete, Greece.

How the Sugarloaf Pineapple became the Champagne of Benin. (2022, February 17). *The Economist.* https://www.economist.com/middle-east-and-africa/2022/02/19/how-the-sugarloaf-pineapple-became-the-champagne-of-benin

48 Jamaica Jerk

The "Jamaica Jerk" geographical indication (GI) is certainly the most popular in Jamaica. The term "jerk" is generally used to designate the historical process of cooking meat, poultry, fish, or vegetables. It traditionally refers to not only the cooking process but the seasoning of meat; a technique which is attributed to the Tainos and Maroons, ancient people of Jamaica. Nowadays, the expression "Jamaica Jerk" refers to sauces and dry seasonings which are currently on the market locally and internationally.

The Jamaica Jerk brand earned its GI status because of the historical link of the process to the territory of Jamaica as well as the ingredients which are primarily homegrown. For instance, Jamaican allspice is one major ingredient found in a variety of jerk seasonings. It gives the seasoning a distinct, smoky flavor that cannot be replicated in other areas of the world. The quality of the Jamaican allspice berry contributes to its flavor profile and to the homey taste of jerk seasonings. The Jamaican scotch bonnet pepper is also essential in achieving the taste of jerk seasonings. The combination of the Jamaican allspice berry and the Jamaican scotch bonnet pepper creates a one-of-a-kind sauce. Therefore, ingredients such as the aforementioned that are grown in Jamaica provide an earthy taste to the sauces and dry seasoning.

The application for "Jamaica Jerk" GI was filed in 2014 at the local Intellectual Property Office by the Jamaica Jerk Producers Association Limited (JJPA). JJPA's main aim was to set standards and establish a code of practice for the manufacturing of Jamaica Jerk. The application was successful, and the term was registered in 2015.

According to the specifications for jerk seasoning and sauce, the list of ingredients that said products are expected to comprise include:

pimento (allspice), escallion, thyme, cayenne pepper, any approved acidifier (e.g. citric acid, vinegar or acetic acid) and salt. Optional ingredients include: an approved chemical preservative, a flavor enhancer, sugar, black/white pepper, and garlic, onion or other spices.

DOI: 10.4324/9781003433675-57

The specifications also provide details on preparation and processing, noting that raw materials must be clean and of food-grade quality and that the product must have a shelf-life of at least six months based on the processing of the raw materials used. Moreover, the specifications detail the cleansing process of ingredients by insisting on the use of a chlorine dip for washing and the rinsing of the ingredients in potable water. A characteristic that must always be present in jerk seasonings and sauces is its distinct, pungent flavor. Furthermore, the salt content in jerk seasonings should be between 18% and 25%, while the requirements for jerk sauces should contain a minimum of 5%. The acidity in jerk seasonings should be 1.2% and jerk sauces are required to have a minimum acidity of 1.9%. The pH level of both product types should be equal to or less than 4.0. There are also microbiological requirements for both product types.

"Jamaica Jerk" is the first geographical expression to be protected as a GI in the Caribbean. There are currently negotiations underway, in the context of the CARIFORUM-European Partnership Agreement, that could facilitate the registration of "Jamaica Jerk" as a GI within the European Union (EU). The GI protection of this term in Europe (perhaps not only in the EU, but also in the United Kingdom, where hundreds of thousands of people from the Jamaican diaspora and their descendants live) would offer JJPA opportunities to further penetrate the European market, thereby also increasing the visibility of Jamaican gastronomic culture at the international level.

The international protection of "Jamaica Jerk" is even more important if we consider the many attempts at misappropriating and capitalizing on the attractiveness of the term "jerk" by people who have nothing to do with Jamaican gastronomic heritage. For example, when Jamie Oliver, a popular British chef and restaurateur, referred to one of his creations as "Punchy Jerk Rice," angry comments were voiced within Caribbean, and in particular Jamaican, communities in the United Kingdom. The diatribe was about the chef's use of the term "jerk" in describing his dish which obviously neither came from Jamaica nor had any relation to the Caribbean island beyond "jerk" being used as the descriptor for the flavor of a microwavable rice dish. What is certain is that if the British chef had labeled his product as "Punchy Jamaica Jerk Rice" and marketed it in Jamaica, he would have infringed GI rights owned by JJPA.

Sources

Bonadio, E., & Poyser, C. (2021). Protecting Jamaican geographical indications: The cases of "Jamaica Jerk", "Jamaica Rum" and "Blue Mountain coffee." *European Intellectual Property Review, 5.* http://dx.doi.org/10.2139/ssrn.3803854

Bureau of Standards Jamaica. Section 3(1) *Jamaican Standard Specification for Jerk Seasoning and Jerk Sauce.* Page 1 JS 215: 1998.

49 Demerara Rum

Demerara Rum is a strongly flavored, traditionally dark and sweet rum produced on the low coastal plains of Demerara, a province in Guyana, in the South American continent. It was granted Protected Geographical Indication (PGI) status in the European Union (EU) in April 2021, being the first geographical indication (GI) in Guyana and the Caribbean to have such sought-after European protection. The term also received a national GI title in Guyana. The GI titles are owned by Demerara Distillers Limited (DDL), a publicly owned company based in the Guyanese capital Georgetown, which is famous for the El Dorado Rum brand.

The Demerara Rum GI published by the EU provides for five tiers of rum: (1) Demerara Rum; (2) Old Demerara Rum; (3) Cask Aged Demerara Rum; (4) Special Reserve Demerara Rum; and (5) Grand Special Reserve Demerara Rum. As far as the Demerara Rum and Old Demerara Rum are concerned, the aging process can occur outside the designated area—these rums having been aged in Europe for a long time. On the other hand, the last three categories require aging to take place in the designated geographical region in Guyana. The EU PGI title emphasizes the importance of such a local area:

> [t]he requirement for Cask Aged Demerara Rums, Special Reserve Demerara Rums and Grand Special Reserve Demerara Rums to not only be fermented, distilled and aged in Demerara, but to also be blended and bottled there, is to safeguard the reputational and historical integrity of the premium and super-premium value, which can only result from the local knowledge and techniques of the production process.

The PGI specifications highlight the local area's tropical environment, the conventional production methods, and the ground water's abundance in minerals. These elements come together to produce the distinctive high-congener flavor of Demerara Rum, which includes "hints of sugar-cane sweetness," fruity and floral notes (from the fermentation and distillation processes), and age-derived aromatics (such as nutty, spicy, woody, herbal, or earthy aromas).

DOI: 10.4324/9781003433675-58

The "tropical" element seems to be crucial here. The PGI specifications indeed reveal that tropical climatic conditions, with consistently high temperature and humidity throughout the year, decisively contribute to a much faster maturation (two or three times the standard one for rum). This specific process conveys to Demerara rums a more mature character compared to other rums, that is: smoothness, complexity of flavors, and rich aromas. Another characteristic element is the altitude. The Demerara region stands below sea level, on the coast of the Atlantic Ocean: it is exposed to northeast sea breezes, which spread the microflora across low-lying coastal areas and naturally provide ventilation to the storage facilities during the fermentation process.

There are hopes that the GI title will give this alcoholic product a major boost in the European market and beyond. The Chair of the DDL Group of Companies, Komal Samaroo, is optimistic in this regard, being convinced that GI protection will help fight the many cases of brand imitation. He noted back in 2017, after having secured the Guyana national GI title:

> [w]e have succeeded in securing the registration of Demerara Rum as the Geographical Indication to be used only for rums produced in the Demerara region of Guyana. The registration will prevent others from using our origin to pass off their product because there is a lot of that taking place. As you create premium value and premium image, there is a whole set of fake products that try to capitalise on your brand and we are very conscious of this and we have seen it happening.

Sources

Statement from Demerara Distillers Limited on Demerara Rum GI. https://demeraradistillers.com/images/pdf/60f5f98953d43-demerara-rum-gi.pdf

Demerara Rum brand becomes first GI registered rum in Caribbean. *Guyana Times*, July 22, 2017.

MAIN SPECIFICATIONS 'DEMERARA RUM.' File number: PGI-GY-02423 – 28.6.2018.

50 Café de Colombia

Colombia is one of the biggest coffee manufacturers in the world and has a long history of coffee making. It is currently the third biggest coffee manufacturer behind Brazil and Vietnam, with coffee representing 15% of the national agriculture gross domestic product. Coffee is grown in Colombia on land between 1,300 and 2,000 m above sea level. Its plantations currently occupy more than one million hectares with an annual production of about twelve million bags. Coffee appeared in this Latin American country in the 18th century—it was first brought by Jesuits and gradually became one of its most significant agricultural products. The Colombian Coffee Federation was established in 1927 with a view to managing and supervising the production and distribution of Colombian coffee.

Due to an oversupply on the global market in the late 1950s, Colombian coffee's price fell from US$0.85 to $0.45 a pound. The market was dominated by coffee roasters who, in order to allow themselves the flexibility to maximize their profit margins, would combine coffee beans from numerous unnamed sources in their goods. Just a few people therefore were aware of the origin of the coffee. The biggest coffee market at the time, the United States, had only 4% of consumers who knew that Colombia manufactured coffee and this needed to change, according to the Colombian Coffee Federation. It came to the conclusion that the issue could only be solved if customers were aware of the origin of their coffee.

For these reasons the Federation started planning and implementing a strategy of coffee branding aimed at penetrating the national and international markets. The creation of Juan Valdez, a fictional character with a sombrero leading his mule Conchita, was a pivotal moment, with such a character representing the typical Colombian coffee producer. An advertising campaign focusing on Juan Valdez was used by the Federation, also in the United States, to increase the renown of Colombian coffee. The result was an increased prominence all over the world. Moreover, it is interesting to note that the strong coffee culture of this South American state was formally acknowledged in 2011 when UNESCO declared the Colombian Coffee Cultural Landscape a World Heritage Site.

DOI: 10.4324/9781003433675-59

What about geographical indication (GI) protection? In 2004, the Colombian Coffee Federation applied for the national registration of "Café de Colombia" as a GI, which was granted. The name is also protected as a GI in the Andean Community, which includes Bolivia, Peru, and Ecuador. Then in 2005, the Federation also filed an application with the European Commission to register the same term as a European Union (EU) Protected Geographical Indication (PGI), which was accepted in 2007—it was the first agri-food product from a non-EU country to receive such protection in the EU. The PGI title has been successfully enforced. For example, when an application for an EU trademark "Colombueno" was filed by a company in relation to food and drink services, the Colombian Coffee Federation successfully opposed it at the EU Intellectual Property Office. Indeed, in 2015, the latter found that a food store called "Colombueno" would likely confuse consumers who may be led to believe that the restaurant serves Café de Colombia as well.

The Colombian Coffee Federation is also the owner of trademarks all over the world, including "Juan Valdez" and "100% Colombian coffee" which have been registered in the United States since 1959 and 1960, respectively. Other registered trademarks owned by the Federation are Juan O'Clock, Variedad Castillo, Regional Caldas, Emerald Mountain, and Buendia. In 2022, the Federation also launched a campaign to promote domestic consumption of 100% Colombian coffee. The campaign is called "Look for the Triangle of Colombian Coffee Quality" and aims to help potential buyers better identify 100% Colombian coffee packaging, which in turn aims to contribute to raising domestic consumption. The Café de Colombia triangular logo is a seal that guarantees that the content of the package is 100% Colombian coffee, produced with the highest standards, and not mixed with other origins of inferior quality, so that the buyer can better appreciate the unique and exceptional attributes of the product.

Sources

Geographical Indications for Colombian Coffee. https://www.cafedecolombia.com/particulares/geographical-indications-for-colombian-coffee/?lang=en

Cases to Come

The curated collection of 50 cases in this volume provides a comprehensive picture of what happened in the recent past around the globe in matters of food and intellectual property (IP). Starting from the assumption that studying the past is a key asset to suitably facing the future, the collection constitutes a needed document to reflect on how to shape IP frameworks and conversations in the years to come. With one caveat: There are some issues on the horizon that may pose novel types of questions because they relate to new technologies or new applications of existing technologies. We could not include those issues in this volume for lack of sufficient data from the field, e.g., no real-world dispute, or no ruling from a court. Before closing, however, it is worth mentioning a selection of potential cases to come. Specifically, we chose artificial intelligence (AI), non-fungible tokens (NFTs), and the metaverse, as it is likely that IP-related cases and litigations in these domains will soon become relevant, with repercussions that may be felt by the whole food industry.

Online Menus and Food Delivery Services

In order to compete, most restaurants have a website where they display their menus and photographs of their interiors and dishes, as well as their opening hours and location. Because there is a widespread misperception that things uploaded on the Internet are open for use by anybody, this information may occasionally end up on someone else's website.

When third-party meal ordering and delivery platforms were first launched, they only featured the menus of the restaurants with whom they had partnered. For restaurants, this meant increased visibility and consumer exposure in exchange for a tiny percentage of revenue going back to the platform developers. This was an excellent approach for restaurants to raise consumer demand through online ordering and door-to-door delivery.

Because customers are more devoted to their favorite restaurant than to the platform, competition among platforms to sign up additional restaurants has grown. These platforms therefore have begun to add non-partner restaurants

DOI: 10.4324/9781003433675-60

to the list by using AI techniques and website scraping applications. A known case involved *Aj's NY Pizzeria* based in Manhattan and Topeka (Kansas, USA). This case was featured in several news outlets—including the August 26, 2022, episode on "Gigaverse" by Radiolab (WNYC)—and allegedly revealed aggressive tactics used by DoorDash to develop its business base during the COVID-19 pandemic. In a short time span, platforms were able to upload fresh menus to their website without the restaurants' knowledge by taking information from their website, as well as their meal photographs, location, opening hours, and contact information. This, however, introduces the inconvenience of a driver (recruited by these platforms) acting as an intermediary between the client and the restaurant; a driver would have to place an order with a restaurant, pay for it, pick it up, and then deliver it to the actual customer.

Some restaurants choose not to engage with such third-party food ordering and delivery platforms due to the lack of control over the quality of the overall services including packing and delivery. On the other hand, choosing not to collaborate with these platforms may increase the risk of them providing customers with out-of-date menus, contact, and company information (for example, such information may not be updated), resulting in poor customer experiences and reviews.

That said, trademark law is likely to forbid third-party delivery businesses from using protected marks in a way that is likely to cause consumer confusion about the relationship between such a third-party company and the restaurant that owns the trademark. Under certain circumstances, such use of a mark may mislead a consumer as to whether the restaurant is genuinely affiliated with the third-party platform, resulting in trademark infringement. However, if the third-party company's use of the restaurant's mark is unlikely to deceive customers, the use is permitted.

To neutralize risks of trademark infringement, third-party food ordering and delivery firms should avoid making statements on their websites or mobile apps indicating associations with restaurants that did not actually sign up for the platform and its services. Alternatively, third-party firms should openly disclose which restaurants are not partnered on their website so that consumers are aware that their order will be placed through the intermediary and not directly with the restaurant.

Although few restaurants have filed trademark infringement lawsuits against third-party delivery companies that uploaded their menus without the restaurant's permission, there is no established case law in the United States and in other countries on menu scraping yet. If case law is eventually established, it remains to be seen how courts will strike the balance between a restaurant's trademark rights and a third-party food ordering and delivering company's ability to market its services fairly and without deception.

Robots in the Kitchen

The so-called digital food transformation does not involve only food delivery services—it is reshaping food supply chains and food systems more generally (Bigliardi et al., 2022). As a good deal of the IP disputes we surveyed involve the work of chefs and more generally kitchen workers, it comes quite naturally to ask how chefs and restaurants can use AI to come up with culinary creations (Alt, 2021; Berezina et al., 2019). We can thus wonder how the use of food can be optimized with the assistance of dedicated AI tools, by offering original ideas for reusing leftovers, reducing food waste, costs, and human errors. It is also believed that AI can solve the problem of understaffing for most restaurants and monitor and control food storage, thus preventing food waste. Moreover, AI is increasingly used to reduce the time chefs spend in the kitchen and customize eating experiences by looking at client preferences, dietary restrictions, and previous meal histories to create menus and suggestions that are specific for each diner.

An example of food-related AI is ChefGPT, a program developed by Microsoft-backed Open AI. ChefGPT specifically focuses on food vocabulary and can generate dinner selections. One of its distinguishing features is its ability to offer excellent cooking instructions with ingredient lists and step-by-step directions. ChefGPT is promoted as a useful tool for both amateur cooks and professional chefs due to its quick and easy access to a vast amount of cooking expertise and ideas.

ChefGPT is not the only AI tool available to chefs. Another one is "Molecular Cuisine," developed by chef Andoni Aduriz of the Mugarits restaurant, that creates novel flavor and texture pairings using machine learning algorithms. Additionally, a number of fast-food companies have installed self-service kiosks that use AI to personalize menu suggestions and provide tempting meal and beverage suggestions depending on consumer preferences. And what about Moley Robotics? This is an autonomous AI system, which uses two arms to glide along a track mounted on the ceiling and is capable of adjusting temperatures; it has been designed to automate many different cooking processes: using a sink, mixing ingredients and pouring them into pans, and stirring pots. With pre-programmed recipes, it is believed that Moley Robotics can prepare over 5,000 meals at once and clean up afterward (Barakazi, 2022).

Restaurant NFTs

Chefs and restaurants increasingly use non-fungible tokens to secure an additional stream of revenue (Kaczynski & Kominers, 2021). It is believed that NFTs may soon become the mainstream in the food industry. But what is an NFT? "Minting" an NFT involves the creation of a digital token that is encoded with the underlying work that the NFT is associated with. Once minted, the

NFT is available on the blockchain for the public to view. Collecting NFTs (certified and authenticated digital copies of a creation) has now become the new normal. And several chefs and restaurants have not missed this opportunity and have begun to tokenize their food creations. Two of them are Tom Colicchio and Spike Mendelson who recently launched their own NFT collection CHFTY Pizzas, with the purpose of creating and strengthening a community of collectors and fans.

Virtual Restaurants

Virtual restaurants in the metaverse are also gaining ground. In the food sector, these digital spaces aim at enhancing real-world capabilities, such as cooking, managing virtual restaurants, and coming up with new menus and recipes. Such spaces are meant to provide immersive food experiences via new technologies such as augmented reality and virtual reality, making new recipes and even virtual master classes from famous cooks available. Big fast-food chains have also taken advantage of these new technologies. Take McDonald's; it already manages restaurants in the metaverse, where users can order food for online and real-life delivery.

Sources

Alt, R. (2021). Digital transformation in the restaurant industry: Current developments and implications. *Journal of Smart Tourism, 1*(1), 69–74.

Barakazi, M. (2022). The use of robotics in the kitchens of the future: The example of "Moley Robotics." *Journal of Tourism and Gastronomy Studies, 10*(2), 895–905.

Berezina, K., Ciftci, O., & Cobanoglu, C. (2019). Robots, artificial intelligence, and service automation in restaurants. In S. Ivanov & C. Webster (Eds.), *Robots, artificial intelligence, and service automation in travel, tourism and hospitality* (pp. 185–219). Emerald Publishing.

Bigliardi, B., Filippelli, S., Petroni, A., & Tagliente, L. (2022). *The digitalization of supply chain: A review. Procedia Computer Science, 200,* 1806–1815. https://www.sciencedirect.com/science/article/pii/S1877050922003908

Kaczynski, S., & Kominers, S. D. (2021, November 10). How NFTs create value. *Harvard Business Review.*

Epilogue

David S. Forman, Ph.D., J.D.
(Retired Partner, Finnegan)

This comprehensive treatise about the philosophy and intellectual property rights in the world of food will be invaluable for different audiences. It will obviously be essential for lawyers who deal with intellectual property (IP) disputes relating to food. It can serve as a casebook for a law school course to train practitioners in this field. It can be a source of both inspiration and warning for entrepreneurs seeking ways to develop and promote their food products. And it will inform scholars who seek to understand the legal and philosophical underpinnings of the developing food landscape. These issues are more than simply contests between corporations or countries about naming rights. They can have far-reaching consequences for economic development, culture, and social attitudes.

Although the book covers a wide variety of ways that intellectual property can impact the food world, new issues are likely to arise. For example, nation branding can not only stimulate tourism and economic development. It can affect the way the world looks at a country. In the 1990s Peru was seen as a country recovering from painful internal warfare. Through enterprising promotion of its wonderful cuisine, Peru is now widely admired for its food, and the annual fair called Mistura is now the leading food festival in South America. Similarly, Global Thai, a program started in 2002, has populated the world with more than 20,000 Thai restaurants, introducing multitudes to its cuisine. Governments are realizing that branding their nation through their food can not only promote tourism and export of local commodities but can also enhance national prestige. Intellectual property is an important ingredient of nation branding.

Biotechnological science is progressing rapidly. Biotechnology may deliver means for revolutionizing the production and quality of food in ways we cannot imagine. People will increasingly be able to modify plants with new characteristics, but also modify fish and food animals, and even to create meat in vitro from cultured cells. Such engineering of food sources may become vital to adapting to climate change, combating new diseases, and increasing world food production to alleviate hunger. And new technologies other than biotechnology will also play fundamental roles. Examples include vertical farming, aquaculture, hi-tech irrigation, and methods to reduce food waste. Intellectual property will be essential to provide the financial resources and ground rules for developing these fledgling technologies.

A recent phenomenon, at least in America, is the rise of celebrity chefs. They star in their own television shows. Their cookbooks are best-sellers. They want specific dishes to be associated with their name. Their celebrity attracts diners to their restaurants. There is motivation to use every possible form of intellectual property rights to capitalize on the great, but often transient, economic value of fame. Thus, additional kinds of IP may be invoked, such as attempts to copyright recipes and the right of publicity.

Governments are becoming increasingly interested in these issues. State dinners, a traditional tool of diplomacy, are given careful thought to maximize their desired effects. The United States State Department and the foreign ministries of many countries are beginning to train their diplomats in gastrodiplomacy, the use of food as a form of soft power. Just as athletes and musicians are sent abroad by governments to engender goodwill, the United States Chef Corps, in which American chefs traveled abroad to exemplify American food, was a successful approach to promote America's image. Thus, chefs became a brand associated with America's culinary heritage.

The diverse case studies in this book provide examples of ways that intellectual property concepts can be used in the food space and disputes can be resolved. But the philosophical implications must also be considered. All forms of intellectual property are rights to exclude. Those rights can benefit the owners, but also disadvantage and cause harm to the excluded. As shown in Case 32 (Basmati Rice) granting IP rights to one country could cause severe economic harm to the excluded country. At some point the harm to the excluded party may outweigh the importance of the protected party's intangible cultural assets. How much can such equities be considered when intellectual property claims are asserted? Can attributes such as UNESCO's Intangible Cultural Heritage, an honor without any enforcement power, become a form of exclusionary protection?

Food has always had an important role in family life, in national culture, and in the economy. With increasing populations, climate change, and shifting international agendas, intellectual property rights will grow to be even more important. And because some of these rights are new and developing, understanding the philosophy behind them will be essential for proposing rules that are fair and effective. The Bonadio-Borghini book provides a unique and invaluable guide for this field.

Index

For Product Safety Concerns and Information please contact our EU
representative GPSR@taylorandfrancis.com
Taylor & Francis Verlag GmbH, Kaufingerstraße 24, 80331 München, Germany

www.ingramcontent.com/pod-product-compliance
Ingram Content Group UK Ltd.
Pitfield, Milton Keynes, MK11 3LW, UK
UKHW020929280425
457818UK00025B/59